The Internationalization of Japanese Business

Proceedings of the Second Conference of the Euro-Japanese Management Studies Association
London, 12-13 December 1985
Sponsored by Nomura International Ltd, London

Dr. Malcolm Trevor is Chairman of the Euro-Japanese Management Studies Association at the Policy Studies Institute London, Britain's largest independent research institute for the study of economic, industrial and social policies and the institutions thereof.

Malcolm Trevor, Editor

The Internationalization of Japanese Business

European and Japanese Perspectives

Campus Verlag · Frankfurt am Main
Westview Press · Boulder, Colorado

Published in 1987 in the United States by WESTVIEW PRESS
Frederick A. Praeger, Publisher
5500 Central Avenue
Boulder, Colorado 80301

ISBN 3-593-33816-5 Campus Verlag
ISBN 0-8133-0531-4 Westview Press

Library of Congress Cataloging-in-Publication Data
Trevor, Malcolm
The Internationalization of Japanese Business

1. Corporations, Japanese – European Economic Community Countries. 2. Investments, Japanese – European Economic Community Countries. I. Trevor, Malcolm, 1932-
HD 2844.5.I567 1986 338.8'8952'04 87-8186

CIP-Kurztitelaufnahme der Deutschen Bibliothek

The *internationalization of Japanese business* :
European and Japanese perspectives; [London, 12-13 December 1985] /
Malcolm Trevor, ed. – Frankfurt am Main : Campus Verlag ; Boulder, Colorado : Westview Press, 1987.
(Proceedings of the ... conference of the
Euro-Japanese Management Studies Association ;
2)
ISBN 3-593-33816-5 (Campus Verl.)
ISBN 0-8133-0531-4 (Westview Press)
nicht mitget.)

NE: Trevor, Malcolm [Hrsg.]; Euro-Japanese Management Studies Association: Proceedings of the ...

Printed in West Germany

CONTENTS

INTRODUCTION

In December 1984 an international meeting of researchers, managers and scholars was held at the Free University, Berlin. The theme of this conference was 'The Transferability of Japanese Management' and the Proceedings were published as 'Transfer des japanischen Managementsystems' (Express Edition, Berlin. Edited by Professor S-J. Park and Dipl. Pol. H-P Merz).

The following December the same group met again, at the Policy Studies Institute, London, to report on and to discuss 'The Internationalisation of Japanese Business', of which the present volume is the result. The participants came almost equally from Japan, Continental Europe and the UK - a truly international forum. It was formally decided to adopt the title of Euro-Japanese Management Studies Association and to meet regularly at the end of each year at a selected location in Europe or Japan.

It is particularly gratifying that the Association has attracted international support and that our Japanese colleagues have expressed their enthusiasm for holding meetings in Japan. This Euro-Japanese link is very much what the Association is about.

In the meantime, we would like to thank Nomura International Ltd., London, for their sponsorship of the London conference.

We look forward to similarly productive meetings in the future.

Dr Malcolm Trevor
Chairman
Euro-Japanese Management Studies Association
Policy Studies Institute
London 1986

WHAT IS INTERNATIONALISATION ?

Malcolm Trevor
Policy Studies Institute

Overview

One of Japan's best known international managers, Mr Akio Morita of Sony, recently concluded that, 'The best way for Japan to meet its responsibilities as a leader in the Free World is to ensure better management of external relations through internationalisation of Japanese society. Clearly this is the way to promote the national interest'(1).

At an official level, the report on 'Japan in the year 2000'(2) by the Long-Term Outlook Committee of the Economic Planning Agency (EPA), 'Assumed that in a long-term perspective the trend towards internationalisation will further accelerate in force', and that, 'It will become necessary for us to look at all problems from an international point of view. Future progress in internationalisation will not simply expand in quantity but will be different in quality from the advance made thus far'.

The report asserted that the process of internationalisation to date had been 'rather easy to cope with', because it had been mainly in the economic field. But it warned that this state of affairs would not last and that, as internationalisation progressed, 'areas related to Japan's economic society' would be affected: 'Therefore, we must be prepared to see the emergence of a situation in which we will be forced to cope with various difficulties'.

The report then went on to examine the progress of internationalisation in four different fields:

1. The commodities and service trade.
2. Capital transfers.
3. Enterprise management.
4. Information and culture.

The internationalisation of Japanese financial companies is dealt with below by Dr Prindl, who is both a practitioner and an author in this field(3), and will not therefore be discussed at this juncture. From the point of view of the theme of the conference, the focus here is on the third field identified in the report: enterprise management.

The report was frank in stating that, 'The accommodation of Japanese enterprises to past internationalisation has systematically been divided into two parts - domestic and overseas - centreing on the system of controlling local overseas corporate firms by despatching management personnel abroad. However, in establishing genuine overseas business activities, it will be necessary for Japanese enterprises to combine the domestic and overseas sectors into one organic sector and work out an equal management strategy. On that occasion, it will be necessary for them to make good use of non-Japanese staff personnel for the multi-nationalisation of personnel'(4).

The paragraph sums up precisely the heart of the matter, expressed in the contrast with the progress of internationalisation 'mainly in the economic field': what is the relation between the internationalisation of business, in the sense of increasing involvement in overseas markets, and the internationalisation of management and personnel at the level of the Japanese enterprise in Europe or elsewhere? Does the former inevitably lead to the latter and what are the implications for 'Japan's economic society', in other words the structure and style of business, in Japan itself? The intention of the papers that follow is to describe the present situation in a way that will help suggest answers to these questions, bearing in mind that the process of internationalisation is something dynamic and changing.

It is significant that the EPA report sees what it terms 'The Need for the Positive Accommodation of Internationalisation' under three main headings:

1. The confused state of the world economy, which requires the cooperative efforts of Japan and other countries if there is to be an improvement.
2. The dependence of the Japanese economy on overseas sources of raw materials, energy and foodstuffs (and on overseas markets for Japanese exports, although this is not mentioned).
3. The increasing strength of the Japanese economy, which inevitably has a greater impact overseas:

> demanding in turn 'a more positive role than before' aimed at solving problems in a 'multipolarised world'.

Some of the questions are taken up in Professor Kudo's paper below. Having set out the basic reasons for the need for continued progress with internationalisation, based on Japanese integration into the international economy and the desirability of regenerating it, the report pointed out the implications for people and institutions in Japan, including schools, universities etc. and how they would need to adapt themselves. That is not, of course, the main focus here, although education and attitude, how managers see their jobs and how they see and are seen by local colleagues are obviously major factors in the management of Japanese overseas operations; as the paper below on the mutual perceptions of British and Japanese managers shows.

More recently, Mr Yamashita, president of Matsushita Electric Industrial Co. has stated that, 'Japanese corporations can no longer just conduct business in Japan among themselves. Given their huge export volumes and their heavy dependence on foreign markets, companies that fail to follow international norms are bound to run into problems. Matsushita knows full well that local production in the United States is not going to be easy. Production of VTRs by a local work force and in compliance with local practices is going to mean high wage costs and low productivity. In terms of the numbers, our company would be better off producing VTRs in Japan or South Korea. But the issue at stake here is something bigger. Unless Japanese corporations like ours can succeed in the United States under the same conditions as American companies, we will never graduate from the level of Japanese businesses playing by special Japanese rules. Until we can pull this off, our companies will never truly be international'(5).

The issue is particularly significant because of the 'new period of growth over the next decade', which is officially foreseen for the Japanese economy(6). In other words, it is to be expected that Japanese direct investment in Europe will continue to expand, putting the management of local operations increasingly in the spotlight.

The Internationalisation Debate

It is common knowledge that in Japan itself the topic of internationalisation is frequently discussed. A recent issue, for instance, of an English language magazine published by one of

Japan's leading manufacturing companies, with extensive overseas interests, focussed on what it termed the 'international person'(7). The contents included articles on 'Business Personnel on the International Scene', and an expatriate in Japan, as well as on discussion of the 'Trends towards Internationalisation in Japan'. The editors clearly felt that it would not be easy for overseas readers to understand what the topic meant in Japan and so they provided an extra explanation in their introduction:

> The closely related subjects of 'internationalists' and 'internationalisation' are a constant topic of conversation in Japan, and to most Japanese those two terms have very specific meanings. To many of our overseas readers, however, the very effort to discuss 'the international person' may seem somewhat odd ... In the past, a tendency existed in Japan to discuss internationalists in a wholly Japanese context - i.e. by, for, and of the Japanese people. Today, however, it is time to reconsider the past and to stand together with the peoples of the world and consider 'international people' from a global perspective.

In the very next issue(8) the same magazine again devoted almost its entire space to the issues of internationalisation and again the editors began by saying what they thought the requirements were:

> The greening of Japanese companies in the international arena has advanced to the stage of all-out production operations overseas. And the companies that are producing overseas find themselves naturally drawn into much closer relationships with the host countries in which they operate, economically, socially and otherwise. In the process of transferring technology and production systems, **and even management methods** (emphasis added), it will be necessary for Japanese corporations to become more international and to break away from rigid Japanese ways of the past.

The magazine went on to discuss 'The Fusion of International Business', the internationalisation of the Yen, how overseas companies can succeed in the Japanese market, and 'The Birth and Significance of NUMMI', the Toyota-GM joint venture in California using the old GM Fremont plant.

In both issues of this magazine the editors' introduction and the choice of titles and subjects gave an idea of how 'internationalisation' looks from Japan. The analysis, in the last quotation above, for instance, also raises some interesting questions. How far is the internationalisation of management alluded to taking place? How far is it possible - or, to some people, desirable - in a non-Japanese environment? Is there a danger, as voiced by Professor Yoshino and others(9), that if Japanese managers do adapt themselves to what they perceive to be local styles of management they will lose those advantages of organisation and quality etc., that have decisively contributed to their companies' competitive edge in Japan? These are crucial questions for success or failure in the management of overseas operations.

Opinions are naturally divided. A senior economist at the Nomura Resesarch Institute believes that, 'Most important for Japan is that we do away with the special mind-set that pervades our society, typified by sectionalism along vertical lines, a situational approach to issues, and the acceptance of inconsistencies between expressed intentions and true feelings. All this mental baggage will only get in our way as we try to create and run a proper international system'(10).

On the other hand, a prominent manager at Matsushita Electric is, 'Very optimistic about Japan's future, as I firmly believe in the Japanese way of doing things, especially that of using every means, regardless of its appearance or origin, if people believe that that is the way to do it'(11).

Non-Japanese views tend to reflect what is seen as the rather gradual pace of internationalisation. A recent survey of Japan by the London Economist, for example, asserted that although the Japanese economy was becoming increasingly intermingled with others and Japanese companies were becoming more international, nevertheless Japan had 'a split personality': though it did consider that, 'A strong Yen will make Japan export more jobs'(12).

The term used by The Economist was 'timid transnationals'(13). Quantitatively, this referred to the studies carried out by Professor Kobayashi of Keio University for MITI (Ministry of International Trade and Industry) in 1978 and 1985. The latter study was based on a sample of 170 Japanese companies with operations in at least five countries and sales of more than one billion Yen. It was based on eight aspects of the business; including whether international planning was included in the firms' annual and mid-term plans as a whole (Answer: 'The Japanese average is not far behind the Western companies'); whether overseas management was integrated with domestic management

(Answer: overseas management is 'still separate and junior'); and whether local recruits could be promoted within the overall company (Answer: 'Not far at all, though there are signs of some improvement. There is little intention of bringing foreign managers into the head office'). The following table of Professor Kobayashi's 1985 findings shows indeed that promotion of local personnel has the lowest of all scores.

<u>How multinational are Japanese companies that operate internationally?</u>

Scale of 1-5	1978	1985	Future	Western multi-nationals
Planning	3.7	4.0	4.2	4.6
Organisation	2.6	2.6	3.3	4.2
Logistics	2.3	2.3	2.6	5.0
Status of expatriates	3.7	3.6	4.5	5.0
Promotion of locals	1.6	2.3	2.6	4.2
Marketing	2.8	2.8	3.0	2.8
R & D	2.7	2.7	3.0	2.8
Finance	2.6	2.5	3.0	3.7

The table implies that Japanese companies operating overseas, on the scale defined above, are not at present as multinational in the areas investigated as the sample of Western multinationals. It is, of course, fair to point out that the Japanese companies have only recently started down the road to multinationalisation, which companies like Shell, Philips, General Motors or Ford have evolved along over the years, and that the Japanese economy has only recently attained the strength and maturity necessary to underpin multinationals, in the usual European or American sense of the word.

On the other hand, it is more than likely that Professor Kobayashi's figures give an impression of greater multinationalisation on the part of Japanese enterprises than is the case. His study did not include banking and finance: two areas in which, along with the trading companies, there has to date been the highest degree of centralisation; in other words, the greatest degree of control by the head office in Japan and the most limited chances for the integration of domestic and overseas management, or for the promotion of local staff to positions of substantive authority and influence. A comparison of the staffing ratios of expatriate managers and local staff and of the types of position occupied by them at operations in the UK, for example, of Japanese manufacturing or sales companies on the one hand and of Japanese banks, trading companies and most financial companies on the other, soon demonstrates the differences between the two types of sector(14).

These differences were referred to by The Economist, which drew a broad contrast between what it saw as the good and bad sides of Japanese management. The former was identified as 'egalitarian', good at motivating blue collar employees, good at quality control, and succesful in obtaining 'anti-strike' union agreements. In Britain, the cases mentioned were Hitachi and Nissan, while in the United States it was said that the Japanese impact had pushed domestic automobile manufacturers into union agreements that offered more job security in return for less aggressive wage demands - and one could also point to the Japanese impact on quality.

The bad side of Japanese management identified by The Economist was in the managerial or white collar office environment. According to The Economist, Japanese offices 'tend to look and to be a bit of a shambles'. 'Loyalty is prized more than stardom, long hours rather than hard work. This makes it difficult to blend local managers and expatriate Japanese and for a Japanese firm to be multinational in the Western sense with international management'. The argument may overstate the rewards given for 'loyalty', rather than for actual task performance or achievement, but there is little doubt that the often commented on question of working hours does reflect Parkinson's Law ('Work expands to fill the time allotted to it')(15).

At a more general level, a report in The Times commented that although Japanese companies 'penetrate every conceivable commercial activity', and although the Japanese economy has the 'vast trade surpluses' that suggest to many in the Western world that Japan should take more of a leadership role, Japanese 'intellectuals, businessmen and diplomats' do not feel the country is equipped for the sort of proactive role that others increasingly expect. 'Despite Japan's economic success, the country is still shying from the limelight of international affairs', was how The

Times put it(16). The question has an obvious bearing on how far or how fast the process of multinationalisation will go.

Conclusion

In Japan it is not only MITI that has a body that is looking to the future. The Keidanren also has a Committee on Industrial Policy and in a recent article its chairman outlined what he saw as the main features of the changing business environment and the requirements that Japanese managers would have to meet. Internationalisation was prominent among them, although there was more stress on the internationalisation of business per se than on the internationalisation of management(17). The often repeated importance for Japanese industries of avoiding protection was again mentioned.

At a more conceptual level, a well known Japanese writer on the strategic approach to business(18) published a new work based on his concept of the 'Triad'(19) - 'three great market regions - Japan, Europe and the United States (that) dominate the world of multinational business today'. It asserted that, 'Quite simply, global enterprises organised for doing business in the 1960s are out of date', and that companies which have capabilities in each of the three component parts of the Triad are in a good position to become 'effective Triad powers'. Those that do not have these capabilities would be exposed to the risks of a vicious cycle of decline. 'The most significant advantage of becoming a Triad power, however, is not simply to stop this vicious cycle, but to pursue a positive and more offensive strategy. Knowing the basic desires of Triad consumers, the company can come up with a universal product. Or, having come up with a highly competitive basic product at home, it can tailor features and looks to local tastes. And it can market simultaneously to 600 million people'.

The writer sees 'the road to Triad power' in companies becoming 'insiders', whether through wholly-owned subsidiaries, joint ventures or consortia. The example is given of Sony which, with its plant at San Diego, remained untouched by litigation and criticism in the United States over imports of Japanese television sets. The company had achieved recognition by its host country as an 'insider'.

Success as an 'insider' in an overseas environment presupposes 'well established management systems' and 'continuity of management, mostly with home-grown, overseas-trained personnel'; in other words internationalisation. How this is to be achieved is one of the tasks for managers.

As already outlined above, and to be discussed in the different papers below, this task has a number of important aspects. A commonly drawn contrast, for instance, between Japanese and European management styles is the more 'groupish' nature of the former and the more 'individualistic' nature of the latter; as frequently identified by both Japanese and local staff, though their terminology may differ. Such attitudes have deep roots, which managers carry around with them, unconsciously or otherwise. Here it is significant that the Prime Minister's Ad Hoc Council on Educational Reform commented that in Japan, 'Over-emphasis on memorisation, however, has hindered the development of independent and critical thought and creativity among students'(20). These are precisely the sorts of abilities that expatriate managers who face the task of welding together an integrated managerial team in an internationalising company require. From that point of view the Committee's subsequent recommendation of 'developing a culture rich in individuality' is consistent with increasing internationalisation.

The paper started out by quoting the view on internationalisation put forward by the Japanese Economic Planning Agency. Government ministries in Japan do not all necessarily have identical attitudes towards a particular problem than they do in Britain or anywhere else. But it is significant for internationalisation that the 1985 Diplomatic Blue Book published by the Foreign Ministry stated that Japan should, 'Strive to become an international state that is more socially, economically and psychologically open ... The homogeneity of the Japanese people has worked in favour of Japan's post-war recovery and development, but this homogeneity can also give the impression of the exclusiveness of Japanese society. Japan must overcome this exclusiveness'(21).

Whether one thinks of the views of business leaders, such as Mr Morita of Sony or Mr Yamashita of Matsushita, of the Keidanren, of MITI or the Foreign Ministry, they all share the same tendency towards greater internationalisation. How far or how fast major Japanese companies operating internationally will develop multinational management structures and styles, in the normal Western sense of the word, or whether it will prove difficult to move from the internationalisation of business to the internationalisation of personnel is what remains to be seen in the near future.

Notes

(1) 'Japan: where to go from here?' The Japan Times, Tokyo, 12 March 1985.

(2) Economic Planning Agency (EPA), Japan in the Year 2000. Preparing Japan for an Age of Internationalisation, the Aging Society and Maturity, Tokyo, 1983, p.99.

(3) A.R. Prindl, Japanese Finance. A Guide to Banking in Japan, Wiley, Chichester, 1981. See also, for example, Y. Harada, 'Financial Deregulation in Japan: Present State and Outlook for the Future', LTCB Research, No.80, Long-Term Credit Bank, Tokyo, May 1985.

(4) EPA, op.cit., p.103.

(5) T. Yamashita, 'Making VTRs and Friends in the USA', Economic Eye, Vol. 7, No.1, Tokyo, March 1986.

(6) Economic Planning Agency, White Paper on the Economy for fiscal 1985, Tokyo, 15 August 1985, quoted in Japan, No.30, Japanese Embassy, London, 12 September 1985.

(7) Toyota Motor Co., The Wheel Extended. A Toyota Quarterly Review, Vol. XIV, No.3, 1984.

(8) Toyota Motor Co., The Wheel Extended, Vol. XIV, No.4, 1984.

(9) M.Y. Yoshino, Japan's Multinational Enterprises, Harvard University Press, 1976.

(10) Y. Eguchi, 'Japan in the Pacific Age', Japan Echo, Vol. XII, No.1, Tokyo, 1985, p.14.

(11) H. Karatsu, 'US Economy on the Rebound', Oriental Economist, Tokyo, November 1984, p.31.

(12) 'Reaching Out. Japan: A Survey', The Economist, London, 7 December 1985.

(13) cf. M.H. Trevor, Japan's Reluctant Multinationals. Japanese Management at Home and Abroad, Pinter, London, St. Martin's Press, New York, 1983.

(14) cf. M. White and M.H. Trevor, Under Japanese Management. The Experience of British Workers, Heinemann, London, 1983.

(15) The Economist is not the only holder of this view. A more extensive account is: J. Woronoff, Japan's Wasted Workers, Lotus Press, Tokyo, 1981, pp.24-56.

(16) D. Watts, 'The New Japan: Supporting role on the world stage', The Times, London, 31 July 1985.

(17) R. Kawai, 'Paving the Way for the Creative Future Development of Japanese Industries', Keidanren Review, No.93, Tokyo, June 1985.

(18) K. Ohmae, The Mind of the Strategist. Business Planning for Competitive Advantage, Penguin, Harmondsworth, 1982.

(19) K. Ohmae, Triad Power: The Coming Shape of Global Competition, Macmillan, London, 1985.

(20) 'Ad Hoc Council on Educational Reform Stresses Need for More Individuality', Japan, No.332, Japanese Embassy, London, 29 September 1985.

(21) '1985 Diplomatic Blue Book stresses Japan's International Role', Japan, No.333, Japanese Embassy, London, 24 October 1985.

JAPANESE COMPANIES IN THE UK

Malcolm Trevor
Policy Studies Institute

Overview

There are at the time of writing between 450 and 500 Japanese companies of all types and sizes in Britain, though this figure includes small 'representative offices' and is constantly fluctuating, as new companies move in(1). In July 1985 the Japanese Chamber of Commerce in London, primarily an association of the major undertakings, listed 283 member companies: a figure that represents an impressive advance over the 180 members that the Chamber had five years before(2).

As far as Western Europe is concerned, Britain and Germany have about the same total number of companies and the same much smaller number of Japanese companies manufacturing locally. In January 1985 Britain had 32 Japanese manufacturing operations, compared to Germany's 34; but in terms of total Japanese investment between 1951 and 1983, Britain was well ahead, with a figure of US$2.4 billion, compared to Germany's US$925 million(3). It is estimated that Japanese companies in Britain employ about 15,000 people.

According to a Japanese source, there are a number of reasons for Japanese companies to choose the UK(4). Apart from the basic ones, such as the size of the domestic market and the availability of skilled (and fairly cheap) labour etc, a number of specific factors are mentioned. The first is the positive attitude of the government and official bodies towards attracting Japanese investment, together with reliability in fulfilling whatever commitments have been agreed. The second is good industrial relations: something that had not been expected, in view of the UK's poor image in this respect in the Japanese media and among Japanese managers(5). The third is the advantage of English, the first foreign language in Japan. The fourth is the 'follow my leader' effect, at present most conspicuous in Wales, where the success of one company has encouraged others to set up operations in the same area; although this pattern has not yet been repeated in every area where successful Japanese companies are operating. The fifth is government pressure to invest, clearly seen in the Nissan case, as a quid pro quo for market share. As Mr. Oba put it, 'De facto import controls in Europe have driven Japanese companies to come to Britain'. Lastly is what is described as greater Japanese familiarity with Britain and its institutions.

In a previous article, the same writer had dealt with the differing Japanese perceptions of expertise in the commercial and financial sector in the City of London, in comparison with perceptions of the lacklustre performance of British industry(6). When it is considered that there are only some 32 Japanese manufacturing operations in the UK, out of the total of 450-500 already mentioned, it is clear that the manufacturing firms are heavily outnumbered by those in the white collar sectors of commerce, finance, sales, distribution and services. At the same time, the manufacturing companies are the ones that receive the greatest media attention. Several have been widely known through television programmes and, given the problems of British industry in such areas as productivity, quality and managerial competence, their pressure has helped to raise the question whether their management styles offer a way forward for British firms(7).

There is no doubt that the new Nissan venture, for example, has raised considerable expectations. This is partly due to the success that Nissan has already had in the British market, giving the company what might be called 'the charisma of success'; partly due to the continual troubles in the British motor industry since the war; and partly due to the size of the operation and its manner of starting up. Nissan's anticipated phase two is designed to employ a workforce of 2,100 - while Sony's TV tube and assembly plants in Wales, for instance, together account for 1,200 people. The 'single union' agreement with the AUEW (Amalgamated Union of Engineering Workers) is also a milestone for an industry which has had such severe industrial relations problems(8).

The 1985 JETRO survey reported that 60 per cent of the 189 Japanese manufacturing operations in Europe responding were profitable. Although there are technical problems in assessing the success of such enterprises, and the important fact that they are more likely to be geared to long term profitability and growth rather than to the short term aims of many British and American companies, Dunning considers that the performance of the Japanese manufacturers in Britain is on a par with those in Germany, Belgium and Holland, and better than those in France, Spain and Ireland.

Sectoral Differences

The first Japanese banks and trading companies opened branches in London in the late nineteenth century; while the first manufacturing operation, YKK at Runcorn near Liverpool, was established in 1970. The judgement that, 'Most Japanese investment overseas has gone into commerce and finance'(9), remains true and the City of London symbolises this pattern of investment. As well as having the major banks, trading companies, insurance companies and securities companies, it is increasingly a centre for the Japanese regional banks and smaller trading companies that are coming to Europe.

In spite of stereotypes of 'Japanese management' or 'the Japanese company', firms in Japan vary in terms of sector, size, business strategy and type of management style or philosophy as much as firms do in Europe or America. It should therefore be no surprise that there are differences between Japanese firms in Britain, particularly according to sector; while plant visits to companies making the same products reveal differences in strategy and thinking among companies competing in the same sector. This can be most conveniently tested in consumer electronics, the major field for Japanese manufacturers in Britain up to the present time.

The most obvious difference between the sectors is in the staffing ratios. The majority of banks and trading companies in the City of London have an average of one third expatriates; while both in manufacturing and in sales companies there are typically no more than twelve per cent expatriates. Since almost all the expatriates in the City firms are managers, with the exception of a few younger trainees, the implications for the role of local staff in decision-making and authority are significant. To put it briefly, one might say that the City firms are centralised on the head office, from which comes the strategy and the funds. London general managers have a level of authority, above which they must consult the head office. They must also do so in the case of any significant new business.

By comparison, the production operations are more decentralised, at least as regards how the targets are met, even if the targets or overall strategy are set by the corporate headquarters in Japan. Given the lower expatriate ratios, the role of local managers and supervisors in these companies is different from what it normally is in the commercial and financial sector and some local staff, such as personnel professionals hired to keep industrial relations running smoothly, occupy quite important portions, at least in their own fields.

Similar remarks apply to the sales companies, in which local staff with knowledge and experience of the British market play an important part, while purchasing and liaison with the parent company in Japan are typical expatriate responsibilities. Generally speaking, the satisfaction of employees, particularly managers, in manufacturing or sales companies is higher than in commercial or financial companies, largely because of differences in promotion chances, involvement in decision-making, and communication; all of which refer back to expatriate ratios and basic sectoral differences. The exceptional cases are the highly skilled dealers in foreign exchange, securities and other financial products that some City firms have recruited.

The other factor in the different sectors is the difference between the local employees themselves. Broadly speaking, British blue collar workers are less geographically mobile and tend to stay more in their home areas, including when, as in the North East, Merseyside, South Wales etc. employment prospects are poor. They tend to identify their interests more with the group, of workmates for example, and a large part of the proclaimed ideology of industrial trade unions is collectivist.

They are generally less mobile and less ambitious than white collar workers, who are more individualistic and more interested in their own advancement at work. Managers are typically both the most individualistic and most strongly oriented towards their own career path. Thus the further one goes up the occupational scale, the more individualistic British staff become and the higher the expectations are. Managers in particular are mobile both geographically and between firms in search of better chances, rewards and promotion.

The British case therefore presents the paradox of the blue collar worker pattern, with its groupishness and solidarity, being closest to the Japanese pattern. Indeed Japanese managers generally get on well with British workers and are pleasantly surprised to find that the difficulties of militancy etc. that they had expected do not arise. In a television interview in the early 1970's Mr. Minami, then YKK's plant manager at Runcorn, stated that he had experienced no serious difficulties with British workers. In reply to the interviewer's question as to why industrial relations in Britain were not better, he said that in his view the fault lay with British management: in other words, it was a matter of poor leadership.

But individualistic white collar staff, managers and 'professionals' present Japanese managers with problems, which are both unexpected and difficult to handle: individualism and job changing being things that their previous experience has not equipped them to deal with. At the same time, it is clear that Japanese managers and British blue collar employees are not engaged in career competition; while for British and Japanese managers in the same firm there may well be elements of the characteristic multinational problem of how far the senior managerial positions are open to local staff. This is often referred to as the problem of 'localisation'.

From the parent company's point of view there have been worries as to whether local managers, with their propensity to change jobs in search of advancement, can be relied upon to run the operations in the right way and, most importantly, to ensure continuity of performance. After all, it is the parent company's investment and the parent company that will have to support the operation if it gets into difficulties.

Interestingly, this worry is shared by British blue collar workers, several of whom told interviewers that they liked the Japanese style of management and that they feared some British managers were either lukewarm towards it, or would actually go back to 'the bad old days' if the Japanese were to withdraw entirely(10). The main points appreciated by the British shop floor employees were the 'egalitarian' style of management, including the wearing of the same uniform by all grades, the closeness of Japanese managers to the shop floor, and their competence and dedication to the task.

Commonly expressed praise for the willingness and ability of Japanese managers to fix machines and to 'roll up their sleeves' and tackle any job that needed doing, however mundane, pointed to what in the jargon of management textbooks would be called their strong 'task orientation'. The praise of Japanese managers by British workers expressed, either implicitly or sometimes quite explicitly, a corresponding criticism of British managers, who were seen as less devoted to the job and the future of the enterprise as a whole and more orientated towards their own personal careers and status by comparison.

At their best, such Japanese examples in the UK show what can be done by managements that give positive leadership to enterprises on green field sites(11); presupposing of course potentially viable corporate strategies, the right products at the right time and the other ingredients that go to make up business success. Most British workers, who tend to be disillusioned and quick to spot management failings, are impressed by what they see; particularly when Japanese companies emphasise the job security that is important to them. But the motivational effect on British workers of task orientation plus 'egalitarianism' should not be overlooked. As one worker, commenting on the wearing of uniform put it, 'This shows that we are all the same: that we are all working for the same thing'.

Flexibility: generalists versus specialists?
Most Japanese managers assigned to manufacturing operations in Britain know that 'demarcation' is to be avoided; and its avoidance is typically one of the benefits to the company of recognising only one union as the bargaining partner, though employees are of course free to belong to other unions if they wish. The advantages of avoiding demarcation at operator level are obviously, first, the avoidance of potential demarcation disputes between rival unions and, second, the freedom of management to allocate its human resources to different tasks as it judges necessary; either to deal with a temporary emergency or to cope with a change in the market. At operator level, the need of high technology companies to be able to adapt their strategy to rapid technological and market change has been most fully appreciated by the EETPU (Electrical, Electronic, Telecommunication and Plumbing Union), which has produced literature in Japanese and conducted compaigns in Japan designed to attract employers to the UK: signs of sophistication that would be amazing in some British unions.

It was stated above that the 'single union' agreement between Nissan and the AUEW 'breaks new ground'(12) as far as the British motor industry is concerned; although its four main areas of single union bargaining, elimination of grounds for a strike, flexibility and single status were already to be found in agreements reached between the EETPU and electronics companies like Toshiba and Sanyo. Accounts in the British media have tended to focus on what they, less than accurately, describe as 'no-strike agreements', ignoring the significance of flexibility: an unfortunate shortcoming in the case of an industry like the motor industry where demarcation has exacerbated serious operational problems.

The Nissan agreement is essentially forward-looking, concerned not only with the advantages of flexible working practices now but also with the changes that will be needed in the future. According to the labour correspondent of the Financial Times, 'Nissan accepts that at first, it will probably not be possible to begin with the degree of labour flexibility at which it is aiming: such multi-skilled labour is probably unavailable even in a depressed labour market'.

The idea is to have two descriptions for all normal employees -'technician' and 'manufacturing staff' - without detailed job descriptions. Supervisors are to have a wider role than has become the case in many British firms. Training, as shown briefly on British television, is naturally stressed and, in the words of the Financial Times again, 'If there is a break in the production line, it will in the first instance be up to those working on the line to effect repairs'. This may seem obvious but it is at variance with established motor industry demarcation. On the other hand, it does fit in with the modern trend towards job enlargement and job enrichment and, as such is likely to be welcomed by younger employees. It may also have a considerable impact on the inculcation of employee responsibility.

In a general or theoretical way, sometimes explained in over-generalised 'cultural' terminology, there is considerable written evidence of Japanese awareness of demarcation in Western countries. Given the greater importance of Japanese direct investment in the United States than in Europe and the greater Japanese concern with the US since the war, it is not surprising that many comparisons are based on American examples; although the British case is not significantly different in this respect.

One account of American-Japanese differences, for example, stated that, 'An American worker doesn't care even if something goes wrong with the machine next to his. Neither does he wipe an oil stain off the floor... It took us two to three years to change this attitude of American workers.... They draw a clear line between their own work duties and those of 'others'. Honda in the US describes employees as 'automobile assembly workers', with the aim of persuading them to follow flexible working practices. Nissan in the US, 'Spent an enormous amount of energy to get American workers to understand why multi-skilled workers, instead of more-skilled workers, are necessary'. In this respect, the British motor industry is not unique(13).

Another Japanese writer asserts that one of three main differences between Japanese and American organisations, and British would be included here, lies in the way in which people are developed: the Japanese looking for more flexibility, within the overarching company context, and the Americans looking for greater specialisation, which implies the acquisition of expertise that can be transferred from one company to another (14).

The JETRO report on European operations also states in its section on 'labour management problems' that, 'In general, Western European employees dislike having to do the work of other sections once having been assigned to their own sections. Therefore, when trying to introduce a multiple job assignment system as in Japanese companies, it is necessary to design the employment contracts to allow greater leeway in assigning ranges of duties'(15). Fifty-eight out of 119 responding companies replied to the survey that they used some such phase in contracts as, 'The employee shall undertake work other than that in his section when so ordered by management'.

From the point of view of Japanese management, there seems to be in broad terms, 'A difference in focus on generalists as opposed to specialists'(16). But how clear is it that this type of distinction does not only apply at shop floor level but also to local managers?

Following the comments above to the effect that the greatest Japanese anxieties about UK operations, and paradoxically the greatest Japanese successes, are concerned with blue collar workers, it apparently comes as a shock to some Japanese managers that 'functional specialisation' or 'professionalism' among local managers is as strong as the blue collar demarcation they had feared. Whereas Japanese managers were aware of shop floor demarcation and industrial relations problems, and were consequently prepared for difficulties, it appears almost as if they did not expect problems with local managers, except of a 'cultural' or linguistic nature, and were therefore unprepared.

Leaving the question of career competition between local and expatriate managers in international firms out of account, what has been revealed is a basic difference in the theory of organisations and in the practice of careers, against the background of labour market differences. To put it briefly, the

Japanese model of organisation may be fluid, flexible and adaptable to changing circumstances, while the British or American is 'rigid and mechanical and is best suited to a stable environment'(17).

The Japanese model emphasises teamwork and flexibility, and therefore the absence of job descriptions, functional barriers and 'professionalism' in the Anglo-American sense. The British model stresses unambiguously defined job descriptions, clear lines of delegated authority and precise areas of functional authority and answerability. What to a Japanese manager may be a welcome flexibility, which can motivate people in more than one area, may be a deplorable lack of clarity to a British manager, who wants to know where his job begins and ends and what other people's responsibilities are. Japanese complaints about the 'That's not my job' attitude and the 'apathy and lack of initiative' in local staff may be matched by complaints of being unable to get a clear answer to a question, of waiting a long time to get a decision, or of not really knowing what one is supposed to be doing. There is no space to discuss all these problems here but they are connected with the two different types of managerial career and the two different theories of organisation; not to mention two different types of managerial status and values(18).

The latter sometimes cloud managers' views of their colleagues and there is a tendency for both British and Japanese managers, especially in white collar firms, to regard each other's views of what a manager's job is as somewhat mysterious or irrational, based on vaguely apprehended ideas of 'culture'; if not downright awkward. Both expatriates and local managers tend to view each other as stubbornly trying to insist on their own way, whether as 'generalists' or 'professionals'. To some extent such mutual misunderstandings are inevitable in international firms, especially where one or other group has little experience of the other's normal working environment.

In fact one could argue that both are behaving rationally in terms of their normal environment and labour market background. Almost all Japanese companies in the UK are branches of the major Japanese corporations; in which the vast majority of their Japanese mangers will stay until their retirement. Joining a company 'for life' and in effect having to make a successful career in it(19) would appear to make flexibility and a 'generalist' career structure centred on the organisation perfectly rational. Equally, in the British case, where there is not the same expectation of a lifetime of work in a company(20), either on the part of the employee or the employer, it is perfectly rational for a manager to emphasise his functional or 'professional' expertise, which alone can guarantee his value in an external labour market, in which there is more mobility than in Japan; though in the latter case it is, of course, on the increase, even in first class companies(21).

But in Japanese companies in the UK it is only the tip of the iceberg as far as the generalist/specialist or management career problem is concerned that is usually visible. Managers on either side who automatically assume that their colleagues share their own views of the nature of managerial work may well have other experiences. It remains an area of some mutual misperception.

Local Components

The other problem area referred to in the JETRO report on European operations is that of obtaining components locally. In the UK this has been predominantly a problem in the electronics industry but it is becoming increasingly important in the motor industry as well. In the US the advance of Japanese motor component makers, supplying the Big Three US auto makers as well as the Japanese operations has been conspicuous(22). Local components are, of course, also a political issue and meeting EC regulations on local content qualifies products to be sold free of tariffs within the Community. The political aspect has tended to overshadow the other factors in discussions of local component supplies.

According to JETRO's 1983 survey of Japanese manufacturing operations, the UK was near the bottom of the list of countries as a components supplier: sixth out of eight, ahead only of Italy and Ireland. There has been considerable discussion of the problems of quality, delivery and price and three is documented evidence of reject rates higher than what the Japanese electronics companies and others have been used to. On the other hand, makers have pointed to the problems involved in production runs which are a great deal shorter than they would be in Japan, to the difficulty of supplying components for equipment that has been designed in Japan with Japanese-made components in mind and to what have sometimes been claimed to be unnecessarily particular standards(23).

It was said that National Panasonic's managing director visited a hundred possible suppliers, before accepting less than half that number. Some have declined Japanese contracts, others have accepted and then been unable to keep up and others have improved their operations; in such areas, for example, as introducing the ppm (parts per million) approach to quality control and cutting reject rates. One Japanese TV manufacturer reported that reject rates on TV tubes had fallen from 5 per cent to 0.8 per cent, and on cabinets from 10 per cent to 0.5 per cent(24). This is a considerable improvement but still not up to normal standards in Japan. Quality problems have affected all types of bought-in goods, including plastic parts and even cardboard packing cases. At Sanyo's Lowestoft factory in 1983 the managing director had a board with reject rates prominently displayed in the main reception room. Packing cases were by far the worst item, with a staggering rate of 27.5 per cent. This was partly due to manufacturing defects, so that part of what was supposed to be corrugated cardboard had no corrugations, and partly due to carelessness in transport, so that cases not properly covered by a tarpaulin were ruined by heavy rain.

A great deal has been said about the relations between main firms and their suppliers in Japan and, to take a rather exceptional British example, between Marks and Spencer and its suppliers. At one supplier in the UK a senior Japanese manager from the purchasing company created a sensation by working half the night on the machines in order to solve a quality problem(25). Other firms have also helped suppliers to improve their performance, although the amount of assistance has varied.

A vivid account of what it was like for a local firm to supply Japanese companies, with their well known attention to detail, was given by a plastics company, which had upgraded its operations as a result. Among other things, they learned to send the exact quality required - 'If they want 2,000 on a specific day and we send 1,999 they immediately ring and ask for one to be sent by express delivery'. It is this sort of experience that makes local firms think of the details and begin to offer the customer a proper standard of service and there is no doubt that the effect of stringent demands is beneficial in such cases(26).

Conclusion

The official policy of welcoming Japanese inward investment in the UK has been quite successful and the manufacturing operations have stimulated an interest in their managerial policies and practices among the general public, managers and the media to an extent that might not have been expected, given the modest number of enterprises involved. Initial fears of industrial relations difficulties have largely been laid to rest and satisfactory levels of quality achieved. Dunning, for example, concludes that Japanese plants in Britain should be able to achieve 90 to 95 per cent of performance levels in Japan and one may agree with his view that the obstacles to achievement have been more to do with 'inappropriate institutions and unhelpful work attitudes' than some sort of 'cultural gap' or 'innate ability'(27). In short, they refer more to outdated institutions in what is an old industrial society that has to grapple with the problems of modernisation.

Differences between the blue collar and white collar sectors remain quite marked, although the latter is seldom in the public eye. Some managerial problems remain to be tackled and the concentration of interest, including among scholars, of relations between British workers and Japanese managers have partly obscured the questions of relations between British managers and Japanese managers, and their different concepts of the nature of managerial work.

These problems are in turn bound up with the wider question of 'localisation', in other words to what extent management is becoming international.

Mr Yamashita of Matsushita Electric visited the company's plant in Wales on its tenth anniversary in November 1984. After returning to Japan, he made some outspoken comments. 'I called together the Japanese executives in charge of the overseas business and told them how disappointed I was. After ten years, our UK subsidiary should have developed the power to produce its own projects, its own product refinements and to stand on its own feet. Instead, it is still far too dependent on Japan'(28).

Questions are sometimes asked about the establishment of research and development centres by Japanese companies in Europe. Given their generally recent arrival and modest size locally, it is to be expected that it is still early for the establishment of such facilities; yet there are the beginnings of such a movement. On 16th April 1985, for instance, the Aisin Seiki building was opened at Sussex University. It was officially described as the 'core of the company's development centres in Europe, with the aim of developing new products and technology'. The Japanese ambassador saw 'the marriage of a Japanese company and a British campus' as a milestone in Anglo-Japanese industrial collaboration(29).

Some other companies have announced plans for European research and development centres(30) and Canon in particular has been described as, 'One of the most forward looking and dynamic of Japanese companies, ahead of many others in moving overseas. By the end of the century, half of their manufacturing will be outside Japan. Canon's president has stated that, 'Our ultimate objective is to develop integrated companies in Europe, encompassing a full range of activities from R & D to marketing'(31). This 'internationalist' sentiment is matched by a recent survey conducted in Japan by the Keizai Doyukai, according to which 'international sense' was in first place when considering the 'ideal corporate person', both from the employee as well as from the management viewpoint(32).

But day to day operations must grapple with the specific realities of the local environment, such as motivation and communication on the one hand and component problems on the other, and competitive reality rather than vague generalisations will continue to determine the development of Japanese companies in the UK and elsewhere in Europe.

Notes

(1) J.H. Dunning, Japanese Participation in British Industry, Croom Helm, London 1986.
(2) Japanese Chamber of Commerce and Industry in the United Kingdom, List of Members, London, 1985.
(3) Japan External Trade Organisation (JETRO), State of Operations of Japanese (Manufacturing) in Europe, Tokyo, September 1985.
'Sauerkraut and Sukiyaki', The Economist, London, 23 March 1985.
(4) S. Oba, 'Japanese Overseas Investment - Why Britain?, Euro-Asia Business Review, Vol. 4, No.2, INSEAD, May 1985.
(5) Technova Inc., Japanese Direct Investment in the UK: its Possibilities and Problems, Tokyo, 1980.
(6) S. Oba, 'Japanese views of British Business and Industry', Bulletin of the Japan Society of London, No.99, March 1983.
(7) M.H. Trevor, Japanese Industrial Knowledge. Can it help British Industry?, Gower, Aldershot, 1985.
(8) Sir M. Edwardes, Back from the Brink. An Apocalyptic Experience, Pan, London 1984.
(9) 'Survey of Japan', Financial Times, London, 19 September 1983.
(10) M. White and M.H. Trevor, Under Japanese Management. The Experience of British Managers, Heinemann, London, 1983.
(11) See for example: J. Braid, 'Japanese Culture in County Durham', Personnel Management, Vol. 14, No.2, London, March 1982.
M. Davie, 'Nippon in the land of Nye', The Observer, London, 1 May 1983.
(12) P. Bassett, 'AUEW agreement breaks new ground', Financial Times, London, 23 April 1985.
(13) 'Japanese-Style Management on Trial in America', Oriental Economist, Tokyo, September 1983.
(14) A. Okumura, 'Japanese and US Management Methods Compared', Economic Eye, Vol. 5, No.3, Tokyo, September 1984.
(15) Op.cit., pp.34-5.
(16) Okumura, op.cit.
(17) Ibid.

(18) The problems of what 'generalist' and 'specialist' managers might be is taken up at greater length in: M.H. Trevor, J. Schendel and B. Wilpert, The Japanese Management Development System in Britain and Germany. Generalists and Specialists in Japanese Companies Overseas, Pinter, London 1986.

(19) See the comments of Mr. T. Ono, formerly general manger of the London branch of the Sumitomo Bank in J. McLoughlin 'Comfort in Suntory's Happy Song', The Guardian, London, 19 October 1982.

(20) 'Lifetime employment', if employees want it, does exist in Britain, in fact if not in name, in the nationalised industries, not to mention the Civil Service, the Army etc. In the private sector it similarly exists in certain well known large firms and it is not the case that all firms apply rigid 'hire and fire' personnel policies. On the employee's side there is nevertheless an underlying assumption of the possibility of job changing, even at a time of high employment.

(21) N. Hara, 'Elites shun lifetime loyalties', Financial Times, London, 4 April 1986.

(22) K. Tomisawa, 'The Auto Parts Industry of Japan: Facing the Challenge of International and Technical Innovation', Monthly Economic Review, No.74, Long-Term Credit Bank of Japan, Tokyo, July-August 1984.

(23) Cf. Dunning, op.cit, pp.86-7, 103-39.

(24) Ibid., p.115.

(25) Mr K. Komada, a senior engineering manager at Toshiba, with whom I talked in Japan in 1984.

(26) 'We wondered what on earth had hit us', Financial Times, Management Page, 10 October 1983.

(27) Op.cit., p.98.

(28) A. Hamilton, 'The outposts of an export empire', The Observer, London, 16 June 1985.

(29) Japan, No.332. Japanese Embassy, London, 26 September 1985.

(30) Dunning, op.cit., pp.154-5.

(31) P. Beresford, 'Canon plans float to spike EEC guns', The Sunday Times, London, 27 October 1985.

(32) K. Moroi, (ed.), Corporate Management in the 1990's. The Evaluation of a New Style of Japanese Management, (Summaries), Keizai Doyukai, Tokyo, 1985, p.6.

THE INVESTMENT STRATEGY OF KOREAN TRANSNATIONAL COMPANIES: QUANTITATIVE AND STRUCTURAL ASPECTS AND A TYPOLOGY OF KOREAN MANAGEMENT SYSTEMS. IS KOREA FOLLOWING THE JAPANESE STRATEGY?

Sung-Jo Park,
Free University, Berlin

The ten biggest enterprises in Korea (Hyundai, Lucky Gold Star, Samsung, Daewoo, Sunkyung, Hankuk Hwayak, Ssangyong, Tusan, and Kolan) stated in their 1986 New Year's messages that they intended to increasingly expand their overseas activities and investments in the future(1).

Two years ago, the periodical World Development(2) brought the NIC's foreign investments to light. Since then, the author has been considerably interested in catching up with the activities of Korean companies in foreign countries. Consequently, during a recent stay in Korea (November through December 1985), the author conducted interviews with top managers in the overseas activities departments of Hyundai, Samsung, Daewoo, and Lucky Gold Star. Accordingly, this paper may be regarded as a collection of impressions and suggestions about Korean management systems assembled by the author.

The first Korean undertaking with regard to foreign investment was a project in forestry development in Indonesia in 1968. As shown in Table 1 below, a small number of projects followed this first Indonesian project up to the point of the Oil Crisis in 1973/74. In connection with the Oil Crisis, Korean efforts to be involved in overseas activities became apparent in the 1970's. Particularly, construction projects and trade activities geared toward the Middle East very rapidly became of major importance and were gradually accompanied by manufacturing and mining/resource development activities. The 1980's seem to be characterised mainly by manufacturing activities, which have been seriously affected by the second Oil Crisis, the securing of markets and natural resources, and, in particular, by increasing protectionism in advanced countries(3).

The fact that the quantitative aspect of foreign investment has shown an up-and-down tendency is obviously attributable to the unstable development of the foreign exchange situation and, moreover, to the newly evolving strategy of Korean multinationals. This new strategy aims to shift investment from construction in the Middle East to manufacturing (electronics, cars, etc.) in advanced countries, especially in the USA and Canada(4).

Table 2 indicates that the mining sector's share has steadily ranked at the top, even though it has recently been declining. Also noteworthy is that the construction sector's share has decreased very rapidly, while the manufacturing sector's has remained rather stable and has been increasing.

The trend towards manufacturing investment, as seen in the framework of regional distribution of foreign investment, is clearly symbolic of a shift in investment from the Third World (especially Southeast Asia and the Middle East), toward the advanced countries (the USA, Canada, and European nations). This trend is illustrated in Table 3 below.

The increasing manufacturing investment in advanced countries has been placed primarily in capital - and technology-intensive fabrication and assembly. Particularly the investments carried out by Gold Star Co., Samsung, and Hyundai in the electronics industry(5) are considered to be pioneer projects which are advancing into a highly sophisticated investment area in the USA. This is mainly attributable to increasing protectionism in America. In contrast, labor-intensive and resource-oriented investment has been made by Korea in Third World countries such as Indonesia, Malaysia, the Philippines, Thailand, etc. This aspect of the pattern of Korea foreign investment is very similar to that of Japanese foreign investment.

Before discussing Korean management practices abroad, mention should first be made of three main points:

First, there is 'no such thing as a typical Korean management system' which may be compared with a Japanese or American or Western European system(6). This is because there was no possibility, in the short period of time since the 1960s for enterprises to work out a sort of 'Korean management system'. For this reason, Korean companies were forced to experiment with two kinds of management systems and to adapt them to local conditions: 1) American management system, and 2) Japanese management system. In practice, Korean companies seem to be extremely **flexible** in putting a mixed form of these two systems into effect, in combination with a somewhat traditional Korean value and attitude system which professes strict central control, authoritarianism, etc. This Korean **managerial flexibility** is fundamentally strengthened by an extremely dynamic, motivated and somewhat aggressive top management which is occupied by young executives trained mainly in the USA, Japan, or in Europe.

Second, when advancing into foreign countries, Korean multinationals enjoy two possibilities for easily acceding to local markets and contacting local authorities. In the USA, there are a great number of Korean immigrants and trainees or US-educated executives. In Europe there exists, in addition to European-trained Korean executives, a solid Korean community of former Korean miners and nurses who came to West Germany in the 1960s. These American and European 'local people' enormously facilitate the adaptation and localisation of Korean companies' management. Furthermore, KOTRA (Korea Trade Centre), SMIPC (Small and Medium Industries Promotion Corporations), and the Korean Traders Association are providing invaluable assistance and consulting services to those companies.

Third, the Korean management system as practised abroad can be considered to be of three types:

1. **Japanese type.** (also termed familistic). The Samsung Group and Gold Star Companies are of this type. They have introduced OJT, the QC System, a limited form of life-time employment, central decision-making, and the practice of placing great emphasis on the 'family symbol' of the company.

2. **Japanese-Korean mixed type.** This form of management is practised mostly in labour-intensive fields in Third World countries such as those in Southeast and South Asia, Africa, and the Middle East. Its main characteristics are a mixture of the familistic approach and some of the motivational and spiritual elements of the so-called 'New Village Movement' (Sae Maul Undong). It is said that the companies' employees are sometimes disciplined and trained in a militaristic way.
3. **Western Type.** This may be typical of Hyundai and Daewoo. Hyundai, whose growth is attributed to the implementation of construction projects abroad, collected considerable project administration experience, and

projects are now usually handled by an automomous decision-unit. Consequently, Hyundai is well experienced in making contracts with particular local residents who cherish a long-term relation with Hyundai. Their local executives in Southeast Asia and in the USA were formally civil servants in high positions. Daewoo, dominated largely by young and highly efficient top managers, was a driving force in the successful implementation of Korean export expansion and diversification strategy. its managerial practice is very similar to that of Hyundai, particularly with regard to the advance into new investment sectors (e.g. car plants) and countries (e.g. Canada, People's Republic of China).

In conclusion, the following remarks, especially those concerning Europe, are noteworthy.

Firstly, Koreans have been hesitant and somewhat reluctant to advance into Europe. Some recent changes are however apparent. It is evident that the four giants, Hyundai, Samsung, Daewoo, and Lucky Gold Star, are increasingly showing interest in European investment, especially because they are facing severe protectionist measures in the USA. The strategy of the Koreans seems comparable to that of the Japanese in the sense that the Koreans are using Great Britain and some southern European countries such as Portugal as test cases before entering markets on the rest of the European continent. In this respect, some Hyundai and Daewoo executives spoke of a '5 years later strategy' after the Japanese had entered the market. Eastern Europe, however, remains a serious problem for Korean companies for political reasons.

Secondly, Korea, on the threshold of becoming an advanced country, cannot expect the tax preferences from EC countries it has enjoyed as an underdeveloped country. Growing nationalistic feelings have resulted in increasing protectionism in some EC countries, especially against the import of 'cheap goods' from the Far East on the one hand, and the rapidly growing capital-intensive and technology-intensive industries in Korea such as electronics, cars, etc. on the other. Such protectionism seems to have led the Koreans to reflect on the future strategy of Korean overseas activities and investments. Several different opinions and viewpoints were presented to the author during his interviews. The start of Samsung's manufacturing investment in Portugal and of other investments in Great Britain and even in West Germany is at present being regarded as a successful beginning; this is especially because, in practice, the 'Korean management system' in Europe has shown a great degree of flexibility and dynamism in localising executives, developing decision-making systems, marketing, and other elements of management. Returning to the original question, 'Is Korea following the Japanese Strategy?', the author would say, 'Yes'. And moreover, the Koreans seem to be more flexible and dynamic than the Japanese.

Notes

(1) Dong-A Ilbo, January 7, 1986.

(2) Periodical World Development, vol. 12, No. 5/6, 1984, p. 505.

(3) For information about the change in overseas strategies in connection with the evolution of Korean development patterns, see S.J. Park, 'The Development of Strategy of Asian NICs: the South Korean Case', a lecture given at the Centre for Development Studies, University of Glasgow, February 1, 1985.
To promote multinationals' overseas activities, the Korean Exim Bank provided extremely favourable credit support as well as an insurance system. For details about this, see Choe Kun Urinaraoe Hae oe tuja Donghyang, 'The Recent Trend of Korean Foreign investment' in Jukan Nae Oe Kyungje, The Weekly Domestic and Overseas Economy, No. 1192, 1984, pp. 12-13.

(4) Dong-A Ilbo, December 19, 1985.

(5) To mention some companies in the USA: Gold Star of America Inc. (Alabama, since 1981), Decision Support Systems Inc. (Santa Clara, since 1983), Tristal Semi-Conductor Inc. (California, since 1983), Samsung Int'l Inc. (New Jersey, since 1983), Hyundai Electronics America (Los Angeles, since 1983).

(6) Christopher Lorenz summarised my lecture on the same topic given December 1985 at the Policy Studies Institute, in the Financial Times, January 3, 1986.

Table 1 The development of Korean foreign investment 1968 - 1985

(unit: 1000,-- US $)

	number of projects	cumulative value
1968 - 1980	287	141.905
1981	34	31.697
1982	31	115.962
1983	49	96.819
1984	15	58.313
1985 (Nov.)	26	20.304
Total	442	465.000

Source: The Federation of Korean Industries, Korean Economic Yearbook 1985 (in Korean), Seoul 1985, p. 174; Dong-A Ilbo, December 19, 1985.

Table 2 The sectoral distribution of Korean foreign investment

(unit: 1 million US $)

	1968-79	1980	1981	1982	1983	1984
Mining	1.4 (1.1)	1.8 (11.6)	10.0 (31.5	89.8 (77.4)	46.0 (47.5)	19.7 (35.2)
Forestry	19.4 (15.3)	-0.1 (-0.6)	11.0 (34.7)	6.9 (5.9)	15.1 (15.6)	5.6 (9.5)
Fisheries	10.2 (8.1)	-1.2 (-7.7)	0.2 (0.6)	-	0.1 (0.1)	0.2 (0.4)
Manufact-uring	21.2 (16.8)	3.8 (24.5)	3.0 (9.5)	5.5 (4.7)	25.5 (26.3)	13.3 (22.5)
Construc-tion	16.9 (13.4)	7.6 (49.0)	-1.5 (-4.7)	7.5 (6.5)	2.6 (2.7)	1.9 (0.3)
Transport	1.9 (1.5)	0.4 (2.6)	0.2 (0.6)	0.2 (0.2)	-	
Trade	24.7 (19.5)	2.7 (17.4)	4.3 (13.6)	5.0 (4.3)	11.4 (11.8)	
Real Estate	15.1 (11.9)	0.5 (3.2)	4.5 (14.2)	-0.1 (-)	-	7.7 (13.0)
Others	15.6 (12.4)	-	-	1.2 (1.0)	-3.9 (-4.0)	10.4 (17.7)
Total	126.4 (100.0)	15.5 (100.0)	31.7 (100.0)	116.0 (100.0)	96.8 (100.0)	58.3 (100.0)

Source: The Federation of Korean Industries, op. cit., p.174.

Table 3 The regional distribution of Korean foreign investment

(unit: 1 million US $)

	1968-79	1980	1981	1982	1983	1984
Southeast	51.3	-0.3	8.9	6.2	25.1	10.4
Asia	(40.6)	(-1.9)	(28.1)	(5.3)	(25.9)	(16.7)
Middle	10.7	10.8	-3.0	7.4	1.9	4.2
East	(8.5)	(69.7)	(-9.5)	(6.4)	(2.0)	(5.9)
North	28.6	3.6	5.5	40.8	41.5	24.6
America	(22.6)	(23.2)	(17.3)	(35.2)	(42.8)	(49.9)
Middle and South	5.2	2.1	10.0	21.7	11.6	5.6
America	(4.1)	(13.5)	(31.5)	(18.7)	(12.0)	(6.8)
	3.9	0.3	1.1	2.1	1.9	1.0
Europe	(3.1)	(1.9)	(3.5)	(1.8)	(2.0)	(2.1)
	24.7	-1.0	-1.6	-3.5	-0.7	9.4
Africa	(19.5)	(-6.4)	(-5.0)	(-3.0)	(-0.7)	(1.9)
	2.0	-	10.8	41.3	15.5	11.6
Oceania	(1.6)		(34.1)	(35.6)	(16.0)	(16.7)
	126.4	15.5	31.7	116.0	96.8	58.3
Total	(100.0)	(100.0)	(100.0)	(100.0)	(100.0)	(100.0)

Source: The Federation of Korean Industries, op. cit., p.174.

THE INTERNATIONALISATION OF THE JAPANESE ECONOMY: THE EXAMPLE OF THE FEDERAL REPUBLIC OF GERMANY

Hans-Peter Merz
Free University, Berlin

In 1984 the Federal Republic of Germany (FRG) attracted 12.6 per cent of the total Japanese investment in Europe. One fifth of the 1984 Japanese production sites are meanwhile located in the FRG. Except for these very rough statistical figures, however, exact data about the structure, size, and development of this investment have been rare, if available at all.

With the support of the German Volkswagen Foundation, a statistical survey of all Japanese subsidiaries in the FRG was carried out in 1984. Some aspects of this study will be presented here; they may be of interest for the discussion about the state of the internationalisation of the Japanese economy and its trends.

Structural development

The development of Japanese direct investment in the FRG by sector is shown in charts I and II. Before 1970, mainly general trading companies established subsidiaries. The first distribution subsidiaries were also established during that time. Banking was of minor importance and production sites were not established at all(1).

The following years until the Oil Shock showed a variety of newly established firms. During that period, most of the banks in our sample were founded, investment rose, and a fairly high number of production sites came into being. Since that time the importance of new direct investment in trading has declined steadily.

Chart II gives an especially good impression of this process. In 1970, over two thirds of all Japanese firms in the FRG were trading companies. This share fell to 38.8 per cent between 1970 and 1974, and has reached a mere 29.8 per cent today. Likewise, Chart II shows the growing relative importance of direct investment in production, which accounted for 15.5 per cent in 1984.

Although there was an essential change in the structure of Japanese direct investment in the FRG in the years between 1971 and 1974, the Japanese foreign economy remains mainly export-oriented. Distribution has grown to be the largest single sector today, followed by trade. While trade - and distribution-related direct investment together accounted for 87.6 per cent before 1970, these two sectors have remained nearly constant in their relative importance (together, around 60 per cent) since the years following 1970.

It is interesting to see how the financial infrastructure of the Japanese direct investment strategy has been brought over to Germany within a rather short period of time. In 1974,, banks and insurance companies accounted for nearly one fifth of all Japanese firms in the FRG. This sector, however, has again reached the relative level of importance which it held in pre-1970 years.

Charts III and IV show the development of the regional distribution of Japanese direct investment in the FRG. Before the 1970s, Japanese firms were concentrated in the area around Düsseldorf, which is still the location for most trading companies today. Hamburg, because of its port, was also of importance for Japanese investors as a location. Between 1970 and 1984, the picture changed dramatically. Due to investment in production sites, which are concentrated in the southern part of the FRG, and the diffusion of the distribution network, all major regions of the FRG are nowadays affected by Japanese direct investment in one way or another.

Control of the subsidiaries

Capital share

Table 1 shows that most Japanese subsidiaries in the FRG are completely owned by Japanese. Fifty-two of the firms which gave exact data about their ownership structure are 80 per cent or more under Japanese capital control. Minority shares of up to 40 per cent are of no importance and will be found only in cases of newly established firms.

Delegation of decision-making competence

Chart V compares the competence of subsidiaries and headquarters for selected areas of decision-making. It indicates that the headquarters' decisions are related mainly to salary structure, introduction of new products, and especially to finance. Decisions of the subsidiaries are mainly centred around distribution, recruitment, and promotion of personnel. This general picture may be differentiated further(2).

Table 2 shows the differences in the decision-making autonomy of pure Japanese firms and joint ventures. Each group was divided into firms with concern-bound and non-concern-bound headquarter companies(3). 'Concern' referring here to 'Keiretsu', or industrial group.

In general, joint ventures have much greater independence from the Japanese partners' headquarters than pure Japanese firms. Of course, this result had to be expected because the influence of the Japanese firm in a joint venture has to be shared with the local partner and therefore decisions will be made mainly on the spot in the FRG. The remaining influence of the Japanese partners of non-concern-bound headquarters in joint ventures concentrates on the introduction of new products (Q* = 0.81) and on financial decisions (Q* = 1.10).

Concern-bound Japanese joint venture partners have fully localised the decision-making process (Q* = 9.00). This tendency can also be found with the purely Japanese controlled subsidiaries which will be described in detail as follows: Compared with joint ventures, the autonomy of pure Japanese companies is significantly lower (Q* = 1.18), but the autonomy of subsidiaries of concern-bound companies is higher than the autonomy of the other firms (Q* = 1.50 vs. 1.00).

So, the decisions for the recruitment of middle management personnel, reorganisation of distribution, promotion, and contracts for supply are predominantly made by the management in the subsidiaries. Table II, however, also shows clearly how the concern-bound companies control their subsidiaries in Germany. Decisions about finance and investment are even more strongly controlled by the concern-bound headquarters than by non-concern bound companies (Q* = 0.21 vs. 0.28).

My hypothesis for explaining the differences in the decision-making autonomy of the four groups described above is the following:

A strategy for the internationalisation of economic activities which relies on joint ventures will strongly emphasise the subsidiary's function of adaptation to local conditions, whereas the decision to establish wholly-owned subsidiaries indicates a stronger emphasis on the function of the integration of business activities into the headquarters' global strategy. Together with the local partners' influence, this would explain the difference between joint ventures and pure Japanese companies.

The different decision-making autonomy between subsidiaries of concern-bound and non-concern-bound headquarters can be explained like this: Concern-bound companies have developed techniques and instruments for controlling and coordinating the activities of various remote departments, subcontractors, and subsidiaries. This strategy will strongly rely on decentralised autonomous decision-making paired with tight control of the finance department. Non-concern-bound companies, however, do not have the necessary experience with decentralised management and tend therefore to overcontrol their foreign subsidiaries.

During the discussion of my lecture, Dr. N. Campbell of the Manchester Business School raised the question whether the differences between the decision-making behaviour of subsidiaries of concern-bound and non-concern-bound companies might be caused by the larger size of the subsidiaries of concern-bound companies.

I scrutinised this very interesting aspect in detail by analysing the relations between autonomy (as calculated by Q* -values), the number of employees, and concern-boundness on the basis of single subsidiaries. Summarising the results, it can be said that the relationship between Q* and the size of a company by number of employees is not at all a linear one. Yet the general tendancy really indicates an increase of autonomy with growing size. And last, in spite of all the exceptions, the decision-making autonomy of the subsidiaries of concern-bound companies is generally higher than that of the non-concern-bound ones.

Control of sections by nationality

While over 50 per cent of all section chiefs in the subsidiaries of non-concern-bound companies surveyed are Japanese, the respective figure for the subsidiaries of concern-bound companies tend more strongly to delegate responsibility to local managers than non-concern-bound companies. This is true with one very important exception - the finance sector is strongly dominated by Japanese at section chief level (57 per cent, see Table III).

This again indicates an internationalisation strategy of concern-bound companies which heavily depends on a mixture of widely delegating responsibilities in most respects and tight control of the subsidiary by means of finance and investment.

Distribution, procurement, and especially personnel affairs are mainly delegated to locals in order to make use of their intimate knowledge of regional markets, the special traits of vocational training, career patterns and legal requirements etc.

Conclusions

Japanese direct investment in the FRG has developed from a trade-dominated structure in the pre-1970 years to a still export-oriented composition of companies by sector. Since 1970, this export orientation has shifted to the distribution sector and at the same time, the structure of Japanese investment has become diversified. A financial sub-system consisting of several banks and insurance companies has been established and production sites have been established in the FRG. Starting from Hamburg and especially Düsseldorf in the early days of Japanese investment, Japanese companies are nowadays to be found in all parts of the FRG. This is mainly due to the establishment of production companies and the enlargement of the distribution network.

Japanese companies have mainly set up fully owned subsidiaries. Joint ventures are of minor importance. Concern-bound companies rely mainly on delegation of decision-making competence to the subsidiaries and to local management personnel. Control is kept mainly via finance -and investment-related decisions; the position of the respective section chief is normally held by a Japanese.

Non-concern-bound companies tend to have a stronger influence from headquarters on their subsidiaries' decisions and sections are generally kept under Japanese control.

Notes

(1) This analysis is based on a questionnaire which was distributed to 550 Japanese firms and information offices, 30 per cent of whom answered. So, strictly speaking, all arguments in this article refer only to 85 firms who took part in the study. The complete results can be found in H.P. Merz/S.J. Park Japanese Management in der Bundesrepublik Deutschland-Strukturen und Strategien, Berlin, 1985.

(2) In the questionnaire, we asked companies to indicate on a 6-point scale whether decisions are mainly made in the head office in Japan (rank '1') or in the subsidiary in the FRG (rank '6'). For comparison, the quotient Q* was calculated by dividing the number of responses of ranks 4-6 through the number of responses of ranks 1-3. In order to more strongly stress the extreme ranks, the number of responses of rank '1' and rank '6' were multiplied by 3 and those of rank '2' and '5' were multiplied by 2:

$$Q^* = \frac{NR6 \times NR5 \times 2 + NR4}{NR1 \times 3 + NR2 \times 2 + NR3}$$

Q* will be greater then 1 if decisions are mainly made in the subsidiary in the FRG.

(3) The decision of concern-boundness was a special item in our questionnaire asking for the self-evaluation of the subsidiary and for the name of the parent company.

Table 1 Japanese share of capital

By sector	0-19%	20-39%	40-59%	60-79%	80-100%
Production	0	1	2	3	6
Trade	1	0	2	0	18
Distribution	0	0	0	2	20
Banking	0	0	0	0	3
Others	0	0	0	0	5
By length of operation	**0-19%**	**20-39%**	**40-59%**	**60-79%**	**80-100%**
Years 0-4	1	0	1	2	14
Years 5-9	0	1	1	1	10
Years 10-14	0	0	2	2	15
Years 15 and more	0	0	0	0	13
By number of employees	**0-19%**	**20-39%**	**40-59%**	**60-79%**	**80-100%**
Up to 75 employees	1	1	3	3	35
more than 75 employees	0	0	1	2	17
Total	**0-19%**	**20-39%**	**40-59%**	**60-79%**	**80-100%**
	1	1	4	5	52

Table 2 Autonomy of decision-making

Q* Values	Pure Japanese companies N = 65 Concern-bound			Joint Ventures N = 19 Concern-bound		
	Yes N = 27	No N = 38	Total	Yes N = 9	No N = 10	Total
Recruitment of middle-level managers	2.50	1.28	1.68	-	10.00	11.50
Introduction of new products	0.76	0.34	0.48	3.25	0.81	1.46
Finance/Investment	0.21	0.28	0.25	6.00	1.10	1.91
Reorganisation of distribution	3.90	2.00	2.58	6.00	4.25	5.00
Salary of Managers	0.74	0.54	0.62	4.50	2.50	3.33
Procurement	2.50	1.57	1.90	10.50	4.25	6.33
Promotion of Lower-Level-Managers	5.27	3.26	3.91	-	12.00	25.50
All categories	1.51	1.00	1.18	9.00	2.89	4.59

Table 3 Leadership of departments in wholly-owned concern-bound Japanese firms

	N.A.	Japanese		German		Joint	
		%	%	%	%	%	%
Distribution	3	6	25.0	9	37.5	9	37.5
		15.3		24.3		33.3	
Finance	1	15	57.0	6	23.5	5	19.5
		38.4		16.2		18.5	
Procurement	4	6	26.0	9	39.1	8	34.7
		15.3		24.3		29.6	
Personnel	1	9	34.6	13	50.0	4	15.3
		23.0		35.1		14.8	
Production	23	3	75.0	0		1	25.0
		76				3.7	
All departments	32	39	37.5	37	35.5	27	26.5
		100		100		100	

N = 27

Table 4 Leadership of departments in wholly-owned non-concern-bound Japanese firms

	N.A.	Japanese		German		Joint	
		%	%	%	%	%	%
Distribution	10	12	42.8	8	28.5	8	28.5
		16.0		22.2		28.5	
Finance	4	21	61.7	7	20.5	6	17.6
		28.0		19.4		21.4	
Procurement	9	15	51.7	7	24.1	7	24.1
		20.0		19.4		25.0	
Personnel	3	20	57.1	11	31.4	4	11.4
		26.6		30.5		14.2	
Production	27	7	53.8	3	23.0	3	23.0
		9.3		8.3		10.1	
All departments	53	75	53.0	36	25.8	28	20.0
		100		100		100	

N = 38

Chart I

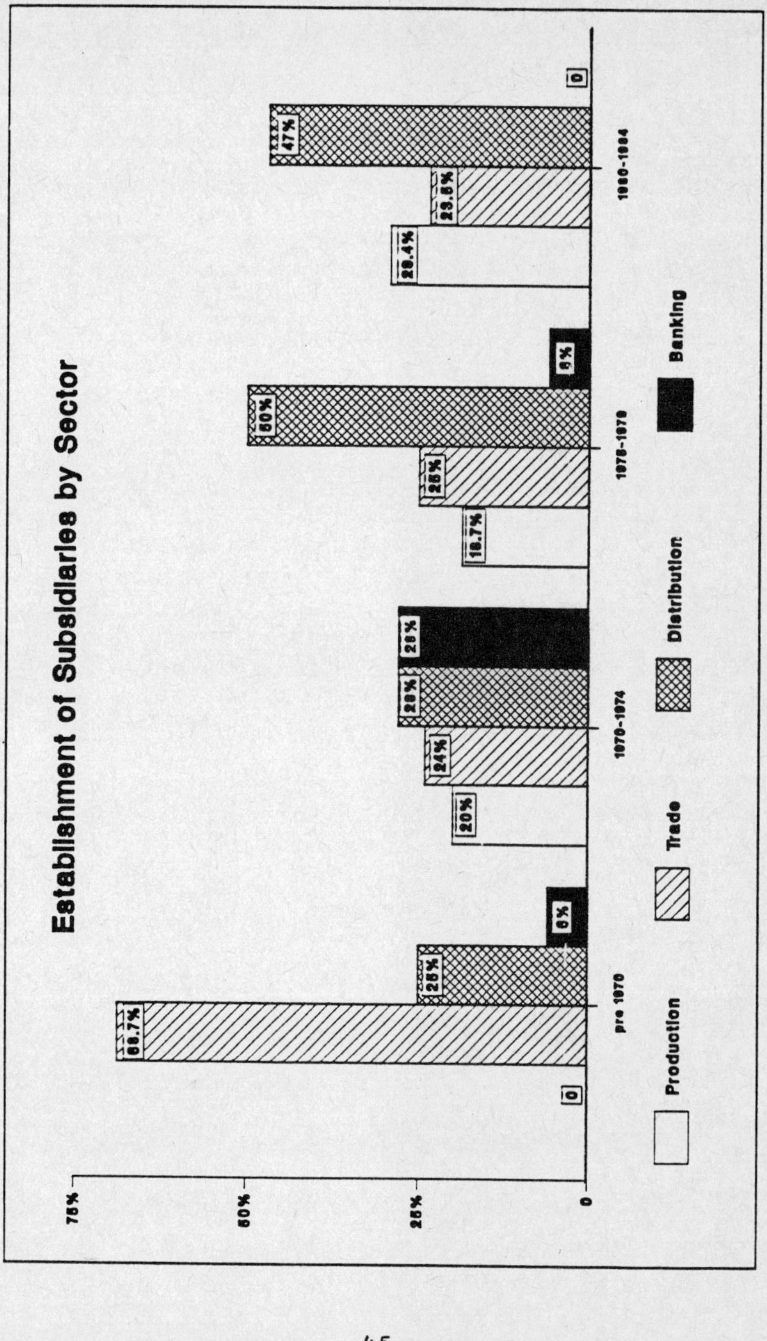
Establishment of Subsidiaries by Sector
75%
50%
25%
0
pre 1970
1970-1974
1975-1979
1980-1984
Production
Trade
Distribution
Banking

Chart II

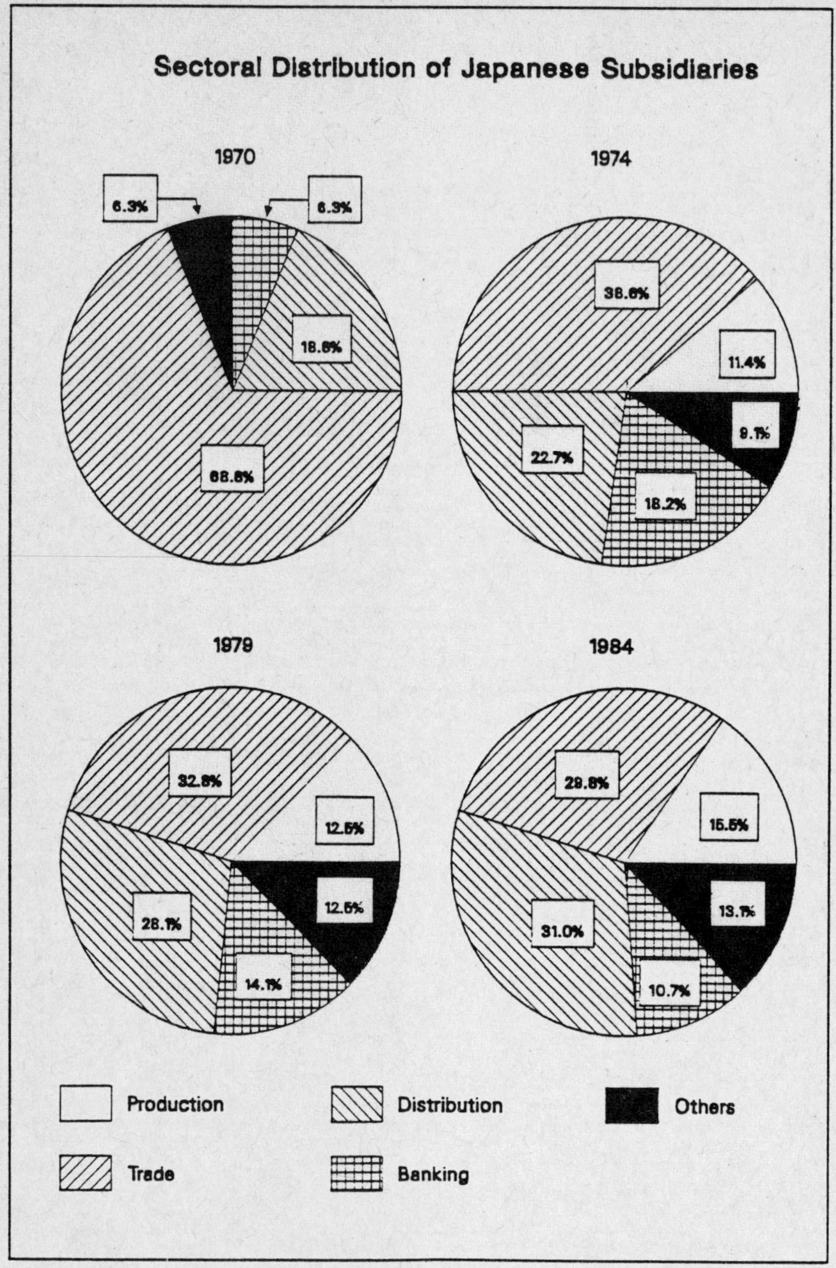

Sectoral Distribution of Japanese Subsidiaries

Chart III

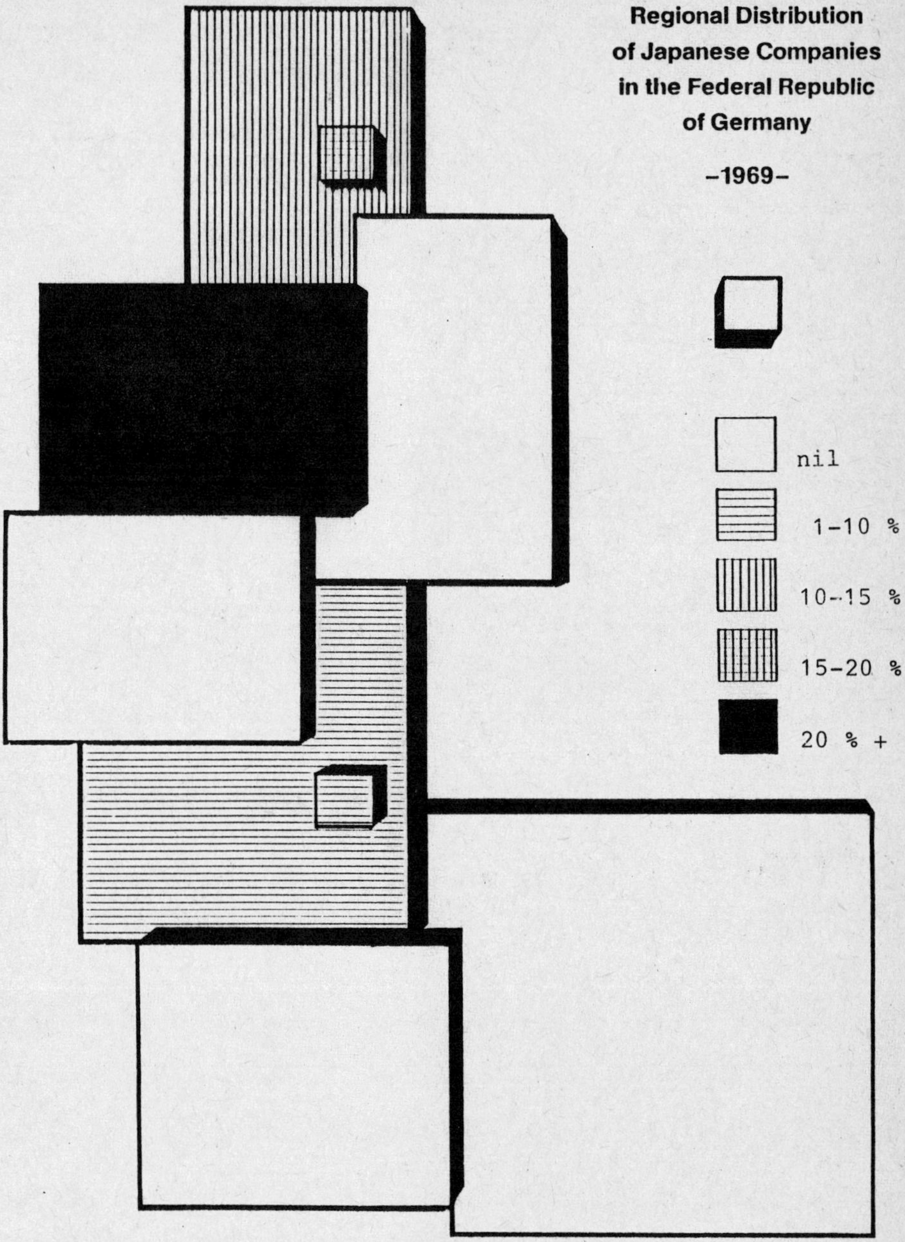

Regional Distribution of Japanese Companies in the Federal Republic of Germany

-1969-

Chart IV

Regional Distribution of Japanese Companies in the Federal Republic of Germany

–1984–

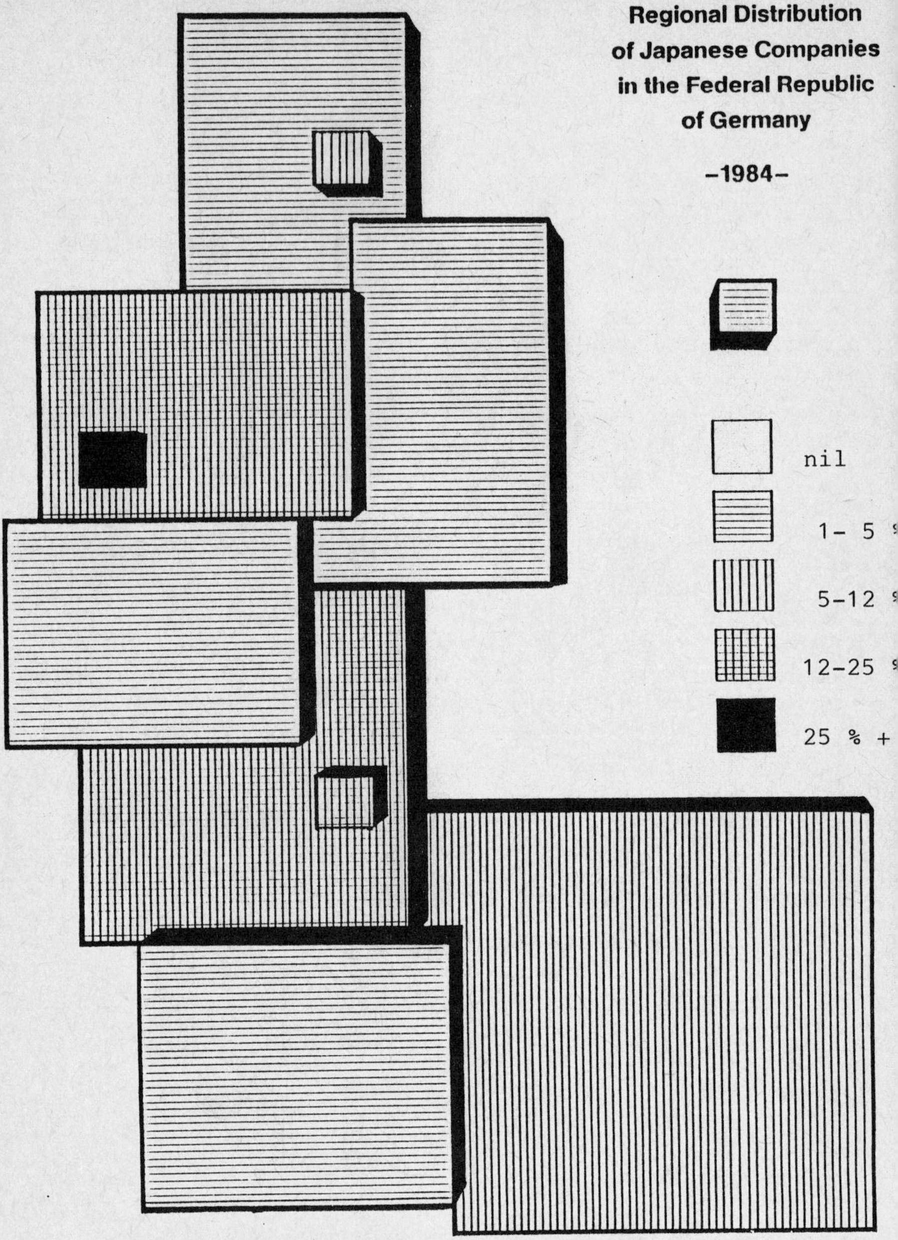

Chart V

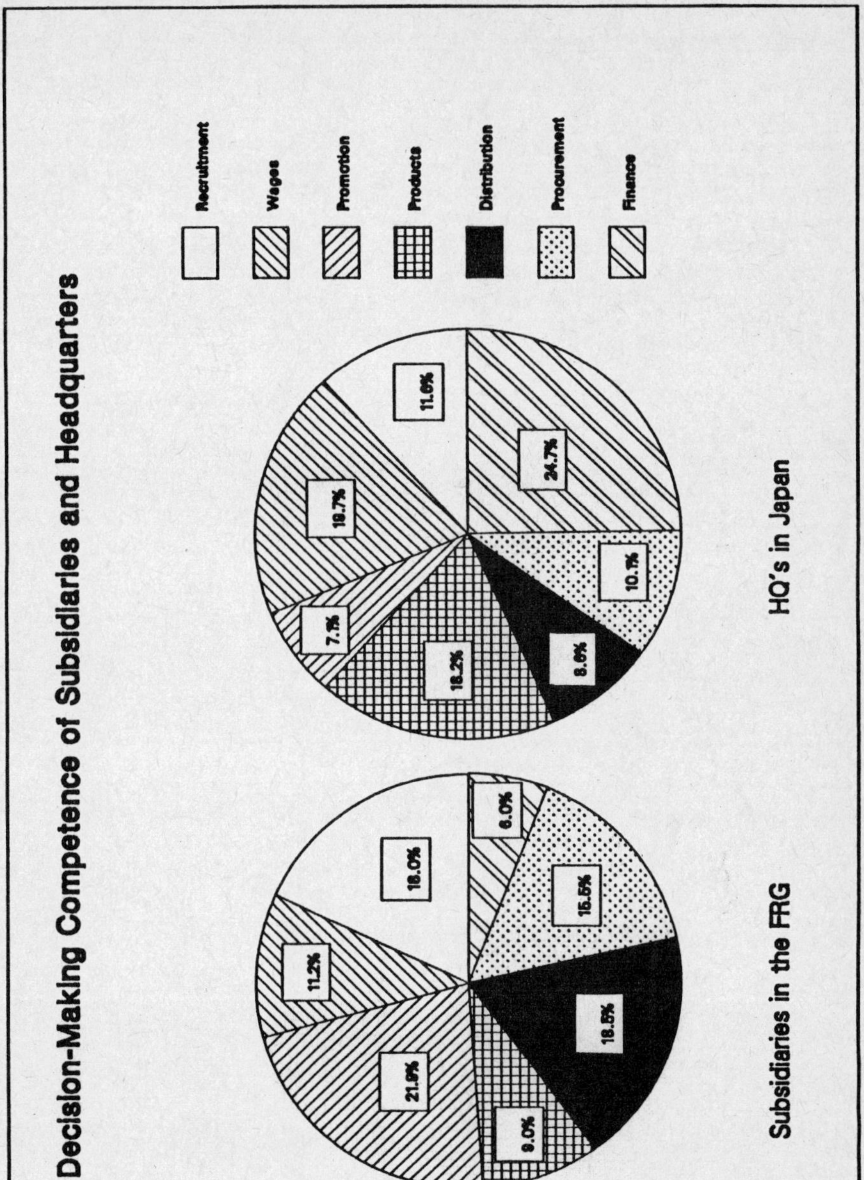

Decision-Making Competence of Subsidiaries and Headquarters
Recruitment
Wages
Promotion
Products
Distribution
Procurement
Finance
11.6%
24.7%
10.1%
8.6%
18.2%
7.1%
19.7%
HQ's in Japan
18.0%
6.0%
15.5%
18.5%
9.0%
21.9%
11.2%
Subsidiaries in the FRG

JAPANESE STRATEGIES FOR SERVING OVERSEAS MARKETS: THE CASE OF ELECTRONICS

F.H. Saelens,
Philips International BV

The evolution of the Japanese electronics industry

After World War II the Japanese electronics industry, like most other manufacturing industries, was in disarray. The stimulus to recovery came when, firstly, the U.S. occupation authorities allowed the production of radios to recommence and secondly, when NHK (Nihon Hoso Kyokai), Japan's official broadcasting organisation, started TV transmissions in 1953(1). From the mid-fifties to the mid-seventies the electronics industry grew at a pace slightly higher than manufacturing in general, and other equipment sectors in particular. Table 1 below exemplifies the growing importance of electronics.

The post-war evolution of Japan's electronics sector can be traced back to several factors. Firstly, spectacular growth in personal income resulted in strong demand for consumer electronics, mainly audio and video equipment. Secondly, Japanese electronics firms found their products readily accepted by overseas consumers, and exports soared. Finally, the government consciously stimulated the growth of the industry.

Consumer electronics spearheaded the industry until the mid-seventies. As Table 2 shows, this particular sub-sector has become highly dependent upon foreign markets, while simultaneously succeeding in keeping import penetration at bay. Domestic demand has, in recent years, been rather stagnant.

In contrast, the demand for industrial electronics has grown at a healthy pace, though in common with the consumer products, much of overall growth is accounted for by export demand.

As Table 3 shows, import penetration has been kept at a steady level while an increasing share of domestic production is destined for foreign markets. The components sub-sector reveals a similar pattern, except that the trends are higher in both the export ratio and the import ratio, which points to growing intra-industry specialisation.

In conclusion, the electronics industry of Japan is rapidly growing and now accounts for about one quarter of all machinery sales. Within the industry, the once leading consumer electronics sector is now facing stagnant domestic demand and has become highly dependent upon foreign markets for its continued viability. The industrial electronics and component sub-sectors have stronger domestic markets but they too have become increasingly dependent on overseas demand.

The Japanese electronics industry not only gained in importance domestically, but also internationally. Whereas in the early sixties Japanese companies accounted for slightly over ten per cent of the sales of the fifty largest electronics firms in the world, by the early eighties their share had risen to about one quarter. Most of this advance had occurred at the expense of U.S. firms.

As noted, Japan's electronics industry has, for historical reasons, shown a strong bias towards consumer products. More recently the components sub-sector has shown considerable impetus. In contrast, as Table 5 shows, the structure of U.S. industry inclines towards industrial electronics, partly due to strong demand for defence equipment. Europe's structure contains well-developed consumer and industrial electronics sub-sectors.

In consumer electronics Europe appears to match Japan but market restrictions in Europe and the U.S., have caused significant shifts of productive capacity from Japan to these regions. Consequently, in terms of ownership, the position of Japan is understated. Japan's major weakness lies in industrial electronics, while her component industry is quite strong. In the long run this latter strength may well prove to be an important asset in the competitive battles for the new, 'digital' consumer-electronics and industrial-electronics equipment markets. These are precisely the markets from which most of the industry's future growth will be derived.

Foreign direct investment (FDI) and exports

Analysis of FDI by the Japanese electronics industry is hampered by the lack of separate statistics. Official data combine electronics and electrical equipment into one industry, 'Electrical machinery'. However, in the course of the author's research almost all data elements encountered referred to investment in electronics, particularly consumer electronics, and more recently, active components. Another author, writing in 1980, also regards FDI in the electrical machinery industry as mainly consisting of investments in consumer electronics(2). Hence, wherever subsequent analyses use official FDI data, they are equated with the electronics industry, rather than the electrical machinery industry as a whole.

Table 6 shows how FDI and exports of electronics equipment have evolved over the last decade.

According to the data the flow of FDI has gradually increased. However, if overseas investment is related to domestic investment, it is clear that since 1976 there has been a steady decline.

The figures of column 2 in Table 6 do not purport to give an exact measure of overseas relative to domestic investment, as nominator and denominator are differently defined. Nevertheless, there can be little doubt about the trend indicated. The table also shows how the export ratio has increased over the same period. Whatever the underlying phenomena, these trends indicate that, in the aggregate, the electronics industry has became **more export-and less FDI-oriented.**

FDI in the electronics industry during the early days was heavily concentrated in Asia, as shown by Table 7. Plants located in Asian NIC's (Newly Industrialising Countries), particularly Taiwan, Korea and Singapore, not only served the local market but also third countries, including Japan. In contrast, factories in less quickly growing economies such as Indonesia, Malaysia and Thailand substituted for imports, as did Japanese plants in Latin America(3).

The factories set up in the Asian NIC's originally produced mostly black and white TVs, while the production of colour TVs was retained in Japan. The NIC subsidiaries were chiefly a locational response to the revaluation of the yen during 1971-1973 and increasing labour costs which rendered exports of black and white TVs from Japan non-competitive vis-a-vis other manufacturers in the Far East, including subsidiaries of American multinationals(4).

As Table 7 shows, the regional distribution of the subsidiaries' sales in 1978 differs considerably from the 1972 composition. Within a period of six years the U.S. climbed from the lowest ranking recipient of FDI to the number one spot while Europe too advanced. This abrupt change was due to the sudden build-up of manufacturing capacity for colour TVs, both in North America and Europe. The regional pattern established in 1978 has not to any great extent changed by 1981.

Japanese FDI in the electronics industry does not perform the same function in every country or region. According to Table 8, sales by manufacturing subsidiaries in North America were originally intended for serving local markets only, although by 1981 some exporting was taking place. In Europe exports to third countries, particularly co-members of the EEC, are not a surprising feature, though the 1972 data look anomalous.

Asian plants were gradually increasing exports, and by 1981 Japan received about one third of them. The remainder went largely to the U.S. and Europe. In short, many Japanese subsidiaries in Asia now function as off-shore supply centres.

Conclusion

Japanese FDI in electronics up to the early eighties is basically a response to two crucial forces. The industry first responded with FDI when its export competitiveness was drastically affected by successive yen revaluations and the labour shortages of the early seventies. Hence, this FDI occurred as a reaction to induced macroeconomic losses in comparative advantage. Overseas investment did not happen across the entire spectrum of the industry, but mainly in those products where cost reduction by technical means seemed no longer feasible or effective. The production of black and white TVs, tape recorders and radios was transferred abroad, but not that of colour TVs. Manufacturers of passive parts also relocated, either in response to the movements of their customers, or because they wanted to safeguard their own cost position. In short, technologically mature, low value added products were transferred to cheap labour locations, particularly Asian NIC's; others were retained at home.

A second force to induce investment abroad was the imposition of import barriers on Japanese consumer electronics, both in less developed and developed regions. Such investment was an important factor in the geographical diversification of overseas production which occurred during the period 1972-1978.

The FDI by the Japanese electronics industry is consistent with its overall development, for example, the upgrading of the domestic production structure towards more technology-intensive, higher value added products, while more mature items are transferred to lower cost locations. FDI in technology-intensive products, if it occurs, is a response to trade restrictions. The preferred mode of serving major foreign markets remains, as in the past, exporting rather than oversea investment.

Notes

(1) J. Baranson, The Japanese Challenge to U.S. Industry, Lexington Books, D.C. Heath & Co., Lexington 1981., p.53

(2) I. Kawahara, 'Internationalisation of Japan's Consumer Electronics Industry', EXIM Review, Vol. 1 No:2 (1980), Tokyo., p.9.

(3) T. Mori (Ed.), Japan's Overseas Investment, Institute of Developing Economics, Tokyo March 1976., p.423.

(4) G. Gregory, 'The Global Electronics Revolution', Sophia International Review, Vol. 4 (1982), Tokyo., p.15.

Table 1 Production value of electronics equipment as percentage of all machinery

Machinery sector	1960	1966	1976	1982	Avg. growth p.a. 1976/1982 (%)
General machinery	31.7	23.5	21.8	19.6	7.3
Electric.machinery	32.5	31.2	31.7	32.9	9.9
(Electronic equipment)	(16.4)	(17.2)	(20.4)	(23.3)	(11.7)
Transport machinery	24.4	27.8	31.8	33.6	10.2
Precision machinery	2.6	3.1	2.9	2.6	7.1
Other	8.8	14.4	11.9	11.3	8.3
Total:(1)	100.0	100.0	100.0	100.0	9.2

Note: 1. May not add because of rounding

Sources: 1. I. Kawahara, 'Internationalisation of Japan's consumer electronics industry' EXIM Review, vol. 1 no: 2, (November 1980)., p.15

2. Electronic Industries Association of Japan, Electronic Industries in Japan, 1983 Edition, Tokyo 1983., p.12

Table 2 Production and demand of consumer electronics equipment

Variable	Unit	1972	1975	1978	1982	Avg. growth p.a. 1972-1982(%)
Domestic production	¥ billion	1545	1613	2216	3523	8.6
Exports	¥ billion	747	946	1387	2518	12.9
Export ratio(1)	%	48.3	58.6	62.6	71.5	
Imports	¥ billion	7	18	22	26	14.0
Import ratio(2)	%	0.9	2.6	2.6	2.5	
Domestic demand	¥ billion	805	685	851	1031	2.5
Comparative advantage(3)	%	47.9	57.5	61.9	70.7	

Notes:
1. Exports/Domestic production
2. Imports/Domestic demand
3. Exports - Imports/Production

Sources: Electronic Industries Association of Japan, Electronic Industries in Japan, various editions

Table 3 Production and demand of industrial electronics equipment

Variable	Unit	1972	1975	1978	1982	Avg. growth p.a. 1972-1982(%)
Domestic production	¥ billion	1225	1580	2316	3933	12.4
Exports	¥ billion	182	340	483	1252	21.3
Export ratio(1)	%	14.9	21.5	20.9	31.8	
Imports	¥ billion	112	172	165	310	10.7
Import ratio(2)	%	9.7	12.2	8.3	10.4	
Domestic demand	¥ billion	1155	1412	1998	2991	10.0
Comparative advantage(3)	%	5.7	10.6	13.7	24.0	

Notes: As for Table 2
Sources: As for Table 2

Table 4 Production and demand of electronic components

Variable	Unit	1972	1975	1978	1982	Avg. growth p.a. 1972-1982(%)
Domestic production	¥ billion	1017	1136	1847	3490	13.1
Exports	¥ billion	217	397	769	1752	23.2
Export ratio(1)	%	21.3	34.9	41.6	50.2	
Imports	¥ billion	59	133	159	330	18.8
Import ratio(2)	%	6.8	15.3	12.9	16.0	
Domestic demand	¥ billion	859	872	1237	2068	9.2
Comparative advantage(3)	%	15.5	23.2	33.0	40.7	

Notes: As for Table 2
Sources: As for Table 2

Table 5 Output composition of electronics equipment in the world's(1) main industrial regions - average for 1981/82 (in %)

Sub-sector	U.S.	Europe	Japan	All regions
Consumer	8.9	27.9	32.2	18.0
Industrial	70.4	54.2	35.9	59.8
Components	20.7	17.9	31.9	22.2
Total	100.0	100.0	100.0	100.0

Note: 1. The data refer to the location of production, not to ownership

Source: Electronic Industries Association of Japan, *Electronic Industries in Japan*, 1983 Edition, Tokyo 1983., p.6 (adapted)

Table 6 FDI, domestic investment and exports in the electronics industry (1): 1972-1982

Year	FDI flow into manufacturing (US $ mil.)	FDI/Domestic Inv.) - in %	Export ratio - In %
1972	69	28	30
1973	156	32	29
1974	99	21	34
1975	96	23	39
1976	164	33	46
1977	161	23	45
1978	243	22	41
1979	180	16	43
1980	309	14	47
1981	475	15	50
1982	267	9	50
Total	2,219	-	-

Note: 1. FDI of 'Electronic Machinery' industry; domestic investment in plant and equipment by 118 major electronics firms; export ratio (exports/domestic production) for entire electronics industry

Sources:
1. Electronic Industries Association of Japan, Electronic Industries in Japan, 1982 Edition, Tokyo 1982
2. Electronic Industries Association of Japan, Electronic Industries in Japan, 1983 Edition, Tokyo 1983
3. Ministry of International Trade and Industry, Japan's Licensed Overseas Investment (various editions)

Table 7 Composition of FDI by region according to sales from overseas manufacturing subsidiaries(%)

Region	1972	1978	1981
Europe	1.1	8.5	4.5
North America	0.3	39.1	40.8
Oceania	1.8	3.1	2.8
Asia	81.7	38.7	39.6
Middle East	0.8	1.0	0.3
Africa	0.9	0.6	0.9
Latin America	13.4	9.1	11.1
Total(1)	100.0	100.0	100.0

Note: 1. Totals may not add because of rounding.

Sources: 1. T. Mori (Ed.), Japan's Overseas Investment, Institute of Developing Economies, Tokyo March 1976
2. Ministry of International Trade and Industry, The Overseas Activities of our Country's Companies, Edition 9, Tokyo 1981
3. Ministry of International Trade and Industry, The Overseas Activities of our Country's Companies, Edition 10/11, Tokyo 1983

Table 8 Destination of sales of overseas manufacturing subsidiaries (%)

A. North America

Destination	1972	1978	1981
Local market	100.0	98.9	97.6
Third countries	0.0	0.9	2.0
Japan	0.0	0.2	0.4
Total	100.0	100.0	100.0

B. Europe

Destination	1972	1978	1981
Local market	0.0	74.5	74.5
Third countries	100.0	25.0	22.8
Japan	0.0	0.5	2.6
Total	100.0	100.0	100.0

C. Asia

Destination	1972	1978	1981
Local market	60.2	58.6	51.6
Third countries	31.7	29.4	32.1
Japan	8.1	12.0	16.2
Total	100.0	100.0	100.0

Notes and sources: As for Table 7.

FROM COMMERCIAL CONTROVERSY TO INDUSTRIAL AND TECHNOLOGICAL COOPERATION BETWEEN JAPAN AND THE EC: THE NEW ROLE OF JAPANESE DIRECT INVESTMENT IN THE EC

Akira Kudo
University of Tokyo

The purpose of this report is to described the history of the economic relations between Japan and the EC from the commercial controversy to industrial and technological cooperation, and to point out the influences of the development of industrial and technological cooperation on Japanese direct investment in the EC.

The Past and Present of the Commercial Controversy between Japan and the EC.

Lessons of the past

As is commonly assumed, at the official level, there have been four culminations in the commercial controversy between Japan and the EC: in 1976-77, 1980, 1982-83 and 1985, although the controversy itself has never been interrupted since the beginning of the 1970s.

The first conflict of 1976-77 is symbolised by the 'Doko-Shock'. In 1980, the second conflict occurred immediately after the second oil crisis, and so-called voluntary restrictions on exports to West Germany were introduced by the Japanese car and TV industries. The third conflict of 1982-83 rapidly compelled the new government of Mr. Nakasone to place restrictions on exports in several industries.

At present, tension is so high that we can find ourselves at the fourth and perhaps highest culmination of controversy. The EC requires from the Japanese government 'a clearly verifiable commitment to a significant, sustained increase in imports into Japan of manufactures and processed agricultural products'(1). The Japanese government thinks that it is endeavouring to increase imports and wishes its endeavour to be recognised enough by the EC. There is a great gap between them.

It is beyond the scope of this report to describe the details of the history of these conflicts(2). Here I would like to confirm only one point: After the second oil crisis, the European economies, including the West German economy, have been suffering secular stagnation and high unemployment rates. Trade inbalances with Japan are persistent. Consequently, in 1982-83 and 1985, the attitude of the EC toward Japan has become stronger than before. But both sides have learnt from experience in the history of commercial controversies and are now exploring a new phase of industrial and technological cooperation.

Steps towards Industrial and Technological Cooperation

The expression 'industrial and technological cooperation' or 'industrial cooperation' or 'technological cooperation' or 'scientific and technological cooperation' is relatively new and is often applied to relationships among developed countries, but it has different meanings depending on the situation. The meaning should be clear in the context of the controversy between Japan and the EC.

The idea of industrial and technological cooperation is said to date back to May 1979, when Etienne Davignon, the vice-president of the EC Commission talked with Masumi Esaki, Minister of MITI, in Tokyo(3). Viscount Davignon was aware of the structural problems of European industries and so was the other vice-president, Wilhelm Haferkamp, who required moderation from Japan and effort from Europe(4), and he intended to revitalise European industries through industrial and technological cooperation with Japan. On the other hand, it is certain that MITI also had this kind of idea and used the words 'industrial cooperation' before their talk(5). In the year 1979, the well known secret report of the EC Commission, which became notorious in Japan, featured Japanese as workaholics in rabbit hutches, but the atmosphere between Japan and the EC was still good in comparison to that in later years. Anyway, the idea of industrial and technological cooperation has not actually been realised. It is worth noticing that in September 1979, four months after Viscount Davignon's visit to Japan, the EC Council took the first step toward the ESPRIT Programme (European Strategic Programme for Research and Development in Information Technologies)(6). It may not be entirely coincidental.

Through 1980 and 1981 few steps were taken towards cooperation.

In October 1981, during his visit to Europe as leader of an economic mission, Yoshihiro Inayama, president of Keidanren, opened his talks everywhere by calling on his European hosts to explore together the promise of 'industrial cooperation', the two-way flow of investment and technology. The European governments and industrial leaders, however, in general however, responded negatively. They concentrated on their own most pressing topic, that is, the menacing growth of Japan's export surplus in Europe and the urgency of holding it in check(7).

In May 1982 the German electric company Grundig opened a campaign for industrial cooperation within the EC and made contact with the EC Commission(8). In October, the Battle of Poitiers took place. Meanwhile, senior EC officials in Tokyo tried to agree with the Japanese government on industrial cooperation in such fields as nuclear fusion, solar energy, nuclear waste disposal and the application of a remote sensing technique for pollution control(9).

In January 1983, the second Japan-EC Symposium in Brussels brought a new phase in the acceleration of industrial cooperation. Sadanori Yamanaka, Minister of MITI and Viscount Davignon agreed to hold regular consultations on this theme. At this time the commercial controversy became overheated. The well known drastic disposition of Mr. Nakasone, which was unexpected by the European side, dated from February 1983, one month after this agreement. Only three months after, in May 1983, the EC Commission made a proposal to require a decision from the Council on the ESPRIT Programme(10). At the same time, the EC Commission was seeking the approval of EC member governments to open negotiations with Japan for a new cooperation agreement in such sectors as thermonuclear fusion, nuclear safety, environmental protection and the development of new energy resources(11).

Consultations were held twice since then, in November 1983 and December 1984. The Japanese side was represented by vice-ministers from MITI and the Science and Technology Agency, and the European side by the General Directors of Directorates-General III (Internal Market and Industrial Affairs) and of DG XII (Science, Research and Development). They took a 'pragmatic approach'(12).

The first consultation was held in November 1983 in Tokyo. It is interesting that in October of that year Nissan's top management definitely decided to produce cars in Britain(13). Both sides, Japan and the EC, exchanged statistical information on research and development with each other, especially in 'high-tech' industries, and on industrial policy, especially in depressed industries such as steel, shipbuilding and textiles. The EC side recognised that the purpose of the consultation was not to negotiate but to exchange information, and that decisions on direct investment depended on private initiatives. However, it hoped for an increase in mutual direct investment, especially in Japanese direct investment in 'high-tech' industries. At the second consultation held in December 1984, they did not only exchange information but also discussed some problems, such as the barriers against direct investment, for example the complicated formulae of the Japanese authorisation system, and the lack of harmonisation in company law and labour law in Europe. MITI proposed to establish a data bank on technologies, which was welcomed by the EC side. It should also be noted here that the ESPRIT Programme rapidly took concrete shape after March 1983, and that the EC Council of ministers for research agreed with the 1985 work programme for the ESPRIT Programme during the second consultation in December 1984(14). It does not seem to me that it was an entire coincidence.

The present state of industrial and technological cooperation

The commercial controversy between Japan and the EC became much sharper in 1985. After a series of Trade Expansion Committee meetings in February and May, Mr. Nakasone's campaign to encourage people to buy more foreign products in March, the High Level Consultation in June, the announcement of the Action Programme and Mr. Nakasone's visit to Europe in July, some hopes on the European side in the first half of this year were disappointed in the second half. The disappointment was greater than before because of increased expectations.

The response of the EC Commission to the Action Programme was negative. An EC press release said, 'The tariff changes now announced are unlikely to bring an immediate or sustained relief to the trade inbalance'(15). The President's conclusions of the EC summit in Milan in June included one item specially relating to the critique of 'Japanese Trade'. In October, the EC Commission published a comprehensive and detailed document relating to 'Japanese Trade' and the Japanese government made quite a tough response.

Regretfully we have to say that this development was unfortunate. In these circumstances, however, the tempo of industrial and technological cooperation is now apparently being accelerated.

First, in May they reached agreement on cooperation in the telecommunications industry(16). Secondly, in the Japan-EC Symposium from the end of September to the beginning of October, Keijiro Murata, MITI minister, made a proposal for industrial and technological cooperation in such fields as electronics, space, atomic energy and aircraft as follows:

(a) MITI would support Japanese enterprises in establishing research institutes in Europe.
(b) MITI would receive researchers from Europe.
(c) MITI would encourage Japanese enterprises to take part in EUREKA.
(d) MITI would cooperate in fostering the European components industries for cars and electronics(17). Furthermore, industrial and technological cooperation was a topic at the first Japan-EC Economic Forum in October and during the visit of the Keidanren mission led by Mr. Inayama in the same month(18). Lastly, at the Ministers' conference held in Tokyo in November, they agreed on the folowing points:

(a) to conclude an agreement for cooperative development in nuclear fusion;
(b) to promote cooperation in the research of biotechnology and new materials;
(c) to promote the exchange of young researchers in the field of advanced technologies; and
(d) to establish a 'Centre for Industrial Cooperation' (a language training centre for European engineers) in Tokyo(19).

In the relations between Japan and the EC countries, we can also find acceleration in the movement towards cooperation. For example, in November, Japan, France, West Germany and the US agreed on cooperation in the field of fine ceramics(20). Japan and West Germany had already reached agreement on scientific and technological cooperation in October 1984. With Great Britain, France and Belgium, Japan has regular consultations. JETRO has already established commissions for industrial cooperation in five EC Countries (Great Britain, France, West Germany, Italy and Belgium)(21).

To summarise, the history of discussions about industrial cooperaiton is not long, and concrete steps towards the realisation of cooperation only began after the culmination of the commercial controversy in 1982-83. Until 1982 there were only discussions at the governmental level. In the course of repeated commercial conflicts in 1982-83, it became insufficient for both sides to depend on the measures used before. There is little room for negotiations and comprises, especially on the Japanese side, but industrial and technological cooperation has become an important way of resolving commercial conflicts.

Some factors affecting the performance of industrial and technological cooperation between Japan and the EC

Interest in cooperation

We consider the following factors as affecting the performance of industrial and technological cooperation: circumstances, interests and capability. Circumstances have changed due to the increased tension in the commercial controversy, and both sides are in circumstances appropriate for cooperation.

Furthermore, it is clear that cooperation can advance the interests of both sides. The Japanese authorities were somewhat indifferent to cooperation in comparison with the EC Commission. They estimated European potential in research and development as lower than that of the US. The Japanese authorities were sceptical about the capability of the EC in mobilising European potential for cooperation with Japan. Therefore, they regarded cooperation with the EC Commission as secondary, and attached more importance to cooperation with individual EC countries.

By now, the Japanese have more interest than scepticism, because they became conscious of the vulnerability of basic research in Japan: the share of the public sector in R & D costs is only one quarter, and the barriers for technology transfer into Japan are becoming higher.

On the other hand, the EC Commission has also become eager to cooperate with Japan at the governmental level, and it has been rather irritated by the slowness of consultation.

Power of mobilising the potential for cooperation

MITI and the Science and Technology Agency (STA) on the Japanese side have many science and research institutions under their control. The newest one is the Centre for the Promotion of Basic Technology Research established in October 1985.

The importance of the government sector in Japan's scientific and technological development is yet to be investigated. Perhaps it is bigger than most Japanese observers assume, and smaller than foreigners usually estimate.

Anyway, MITI and the STA play more important roles in basic studies than in the applied field. They promote basic research that has a future but which is usually financially impossible for private enterprises to support. They have been applying the so called 'big project method' to the promotion of basic research since 1966; that is, MITI plays the role of coordinator, and gathers and systematises knowledge and know-how which has been accumulated in the public sector and by private enterprises. In 1985 MITI started a new 'joint research system of the public and private sectors' (Kanmin rentai kyodo kenkyu seido) and selected 6 research themes. They mapped out as new lines in joint research:

(a) exchange of research results
(b) joint use of equipment, and
(c) joint ownership of industrial property resulting from this joint research(22)

Another example: the Ministry of Post and Telecommunications and the Centre for the Promotion of Basic Technology Research has also decided to promote 5 projects in the field of telecommunications as 'national projects'(23). MITI and other ministries have a tradition of and competence in mobilising private research potential and these systems have been efficient.

The EC had 67 internal projects within the framework of industrial and technological cooperation as of November 1984, in all industries from agriculture to space, in addition to ECSC and EURATOM(24).

In these projects, the EC plays the role of coordinator and financier. Some of them are financed by the EC, some are financed privately and others are financed both by the EC and private companies. For example, in the case of the ESPRIT Programme, private companies choose the technologies to be developed, and the R & D costs are financed by the EC and the private companies on a fifty-fifty basis. This is somewhat different from the 'big project method' in Japan. The EC Commission is now searching for a new way of cooperation(25). Cooperation between Japan and the EC at the governmental level can develop further in the future.

There are, however, some uncertain factors. Among them, one is to be mentioned: the promotion of cooperation within the EC aimed at manufacturing and strengthening European competitiveness against the US and Japan. It is symbolic of the strategy of the EC that the President's conclusions at the EC Milan Summit included the items 'New Technology' and 'Japanese Trade' side by side. This conception of a certain type of technology community can increase the centripetal force of the EC. Only after consolidating cooperation within the EC, can the EC be prepared for cooperation with Japan and the US, as suggested several times before. For example, in the autumn of 1983, when the EC began consultations on cooperation with Japan, the EC also had the strongest will to establish internal cooperation.

On the other hand, EC countries are competing with each

other for cooperation with the US and Japan. They cannot wait for the completion of internal cooperation.

European cooperation goes beyond the institution of the EC, for example the Airbus and Eurofighter, or beyond the territory of the EC, as in EUREKA and the Reunion Round Table(26). These projects are mostly 'Eurocentric'. The first two are apparently closed. Although Mr. Nakasone announced the possibility of Japan's participation in EUREKA(27), this possibility seems to be slight. The Reunion Round Table is entirely exclusive. It may be suggestive that an American enterprise, IBM Europe, is participating in the ESPRIT Programme, while no Japanese enterprise is yet doing so(28).

The following scenario is most probable: France and West Germany will get closer to each other, either in the framework of the EC or beyond it. On this Paris-Bonn Axis, the EC will approach Japan for industrial and technological cooperation despite commercial conflicts. Cooperation between Japan and the EC will follow close on that between Japan and each EC member country. It will take, so to say a, 'de jure approach', like cooperation between Japan and France(29). If EC projects become more centripetal than centrifugal, the participation of Japanese business in EC projects will be limited.

Concluding remarks: the new role of Japanese direct investment in the EC

We have mainly seen a certain type of industrial and technological cooperation, that is, cooperation at the governmental level. Direct investment, the supply of technical licenses and know-how etc. belong to another type of cooperation. Governments cannot promote this type of cooperation under their direction. They find this type of cooperation inadequate but are willing to facilitate it. We now consider the influences of the changes in Japan-EC economic relations on the future course of direct investment, especially on Japanese investment in the EC.

JETRO's second survey of Japanese investment in Europe says: 'In conclusion, the survey result indicates that local manufacturing in Western Europe is not without inherent problems, but that management flexibility has helped smooth out rough corners. In the process, Japanese managers have learned how to deal with local differences and gained confidence in their future in Europe'(30). In reporting this result, most of the Japanese press laid emphasis on the successful introduction or penetration of the Japanese style of management into Japanese enterprises in Europe(31). The EC Commission, on the other hand, criticises Japanese direct investment as follows:

(a) Japanese enterprises are being established mostly in tertiary industries in order to sell Japanese products or to finance Japanese producers, not in order to produce in Europe.
(b) The share of local procurement is considerably lower than the Commission wishes. The often mentioned 'difference in the quality of locally produced parts' is nothing but an excuse.
(c) Transfer of technology from Japan to the EC is insufficient, as seen from Japan's deficit balance of technology.
(d) All in all, Japanese investment in the EC is threatening European industries more than contributing to prosperity, employment and technological development in Europe(32). Reportedly, the EC Commission (DG IV - Competition) is now examining the possibility of laying down guide lines in order to prevent the excessive dominance of joint ventures in the market(33).

How and to what extent can Japanese enterprises in the EC respond to these criticisms by host countries? As one part of industrial and technological cooperation, Japanese direct investment in the EC can and should not only decrease the potentiality of commercial conflicts, but also contribute to the economic prosperity and political stability of Europe through the creation of employment and the transfer of technology to the EC. Here we can realise a new role for Japanese direct investment in the EC.

Notes

(1) EC Council Declaration on EC-Japan Relations, 18 June, 1985.
(2) See Akira Kudo, Handelskontroverse zwischen Japan und der EG, Occasional Papers, East Asian Institute, Free University of Berlin, 1985.
(3) JETRO-Information, Sonderausgabe für industrielle und technische Kooperation, March 1984.
(4) Wilhelm Haferkamp, 'Japan and the European Community: An Uneasy Partnership', Intereconomics, January/February 1981.
(5) The Japan Times, 19 June, 1979.
(6) Yoshikiyo Minami, 'New Development of Research and Development Policy in Information Technologies in the European Communities', EC Studies in Japan, No.5, 1985 (in Japanese), pp.202-3.
(7) The Japan Times, 20 October, 1981.
(8) Minami, op.cit, pp.212-3.
(9) Financial Times, 22 June, 1982. See also The Japan Times, 22 June, 1982.

(10) Minami, op.cit., pp.215-6.
(11) Financial Times, 10 May, 1983.
(12) The following description depends primarily on interviews held in June 1985 with some civil servants of the EC Commission and of Japanese Embassies in the EC. The records of these consultations are confidential.
(13) International Herald Tribune, 24 October, 1983.
(14) Minami, op.cit., p.227.
(15) EC Press Release.
(16) Frankfurter Allgemeine Zeitung, 13 May, 1985
In March 1985 the EC Commission had made a proposal for RACE (R & D in Advanced Communications Technologies for Europe). Minami, op.cit., p.226.
(17) Nihon keizai Shinbun, 29 September, 1985.
(18) Ibid., 3 & 18 October, 1985.
(19) Ibid., 17 & 19 November, 1985.
(20) Ibid., 8 November, 1985. Other examples: Japan, Great Britain, France and the US in the automatic translation telephone; Japan and West Germany in the space Lab project 'D2'; Japan and France in 'Aqua renaissance 90'. Ibid., 23 & 34 November, 1985.
(21) JETRO, op.cit.
(22) Nihon Keizai Shinbun, 28 October, 1985.
(23) Ibid.
(24) Die Forschungspolitik der Europäischen Gemeinschaft, 2nd Edition, 1985, p.42.
(25) Interviews in Brussels.
(26) Participating enterprises are Volvo, Fiat, Olivetti, Philips, Petrofina, the National Coal Board, Awooa, R.T. The President of the EC Commission, Jacques Delors, and other members of the Commission are also participants. EC source.
(27) Frankfurter Allgemeine Zeitung, 12 July, 1985.
(28) Minami, op.cit., p.227.
(29) Cooperation between Japan and each EC country is in progress. France is de jure oriented and Great Britain and West Germany are de facto oriented, for example, in the case of the fifth generation computer. Frankfurter Allgemeine Zeitung, 16 May, 1984 and Nihon Keizai Shinbun, 15 October, 1985.
(30) Japanese investment in Western Europe: a JETRO survey, 1985.
(31) JETRO materials.
(32) Interviews in Brussels.
(33) Nihon Keizai Shinbun, 16 November, 1985.

NISSAN'S INTERNATIONAL STRATEGY

Mitsuya Goto
Nissan Motor Co. Ltd.

Japanese companies have been rather slow in becoming truly international. The move towards internationalisation has been led by YKK, Sony and Honda, and others are trying to follow their lead by investing heavily overseas. There are a lot of Japanese companies nowadays that are feeling growing pains in becoming international or multinational in the true sense of the word.

Japanese companies have been especially slow and reluctant in investing in advanced countries in Europe and North America.

Why have they been so slow and reluctant? Most Japanese companies, having had no international experience, feel uncertain if they are truly welcome in the host country. Even if they do decide to make a direct investment, they will often feel like the 'odd man out' in a cold and foreign environment. They will have certain fears of having to deal with a local trade union or trade unions. They will also have certain concerns in dealing with local parts and component suppliers. And then there will be a language barrier to overcome in communicating with their local managers and employees.

Nevertheless, more Japanese companies should be encouraged to invest overseas and to assume a greater international role.

Our company, Nissan Motor Co., has been pushing internationalisation for some time, and I am sure that you will agree that we are far more international then our major rival, Toyota.

Beginning about 1980, Nissan, under the leadership of the then President, Mr Ishihara, who is now Chairman, expanded internationally. In fact, internationalisation was one of the three major objectives that he set for Nissan.

At that point in time, Nissan had some ten manufacturing plants in Japan, mostly in the greater Tokyo/Yokohama area, and 25 plants in 20 countries outside Japan. Of the 25 plants overseas, only two were our own investments, namely in Mexico and Australia. All the others were built by local capital which had been under license to produce Nissan/Datsun cars for the local market.

Beginning in the 1980s, Mr Ishihara started Nissan on the road to internationalisation or multinationalisation. This is seen in six main ways. First, we set up a 50/50 joint venture with Alfa Romeo of Italy which for some time had been in financial difficulty and looking for a foreign partner. The joint venture, called ARNA, built a body assembly plant near Naples and started building bodies-in-white of a version of the Nissan Cherry. The completed bodies are taken to the nearby Alfasud plant in Pomigliano where they are mated with Alfa Romeo engines and all the innards. Only the body panels are from Japan, so I always say that the car has at least 80 per cent hot Italian blood with a Japanese kimono on it. The Alfa Romeo version went on sale in Italy and the Nissan version went on sale in the UK, Austria, etc.

Second, Nissan acquired 33 per cent of Motor Iberica, the Spanish truck and agricultural tractor manufacturer and later increased our share to 84 per cent, when in 1984 we started production of a Jeep type vehicle, the Nissan Patrol. Later the company started producing a small van, the Nissan Vanette.

Third, we entered into an agreement with Volkswagen of West Germany under which we started producing Volkswagen's Santana model in one of our assembly plants near Tokyo beginning in February in 1984. Nissan now sells 2,000 Santanas a month through its own dealerships in Japan on behalf of Volkswagen. This is mainly to counter the criticism on the part of European and US car manufacturers that the Japanese market is so difficult to penetrate.

Fourth, we have invested US$750 million in Smyrna, Tennessee, to build pick-up trucks there. This is the largest investment ever by a Japanese company in North America. The new plant was completed in the Spring of 1983 and the first truck came off the assembly line in June. This plant now employs 3,000 people, mostly Tennesseans, and produces 240,000 pick-up trucks and cars a year. The State of Tennessee had set aside US$7.3 million for pre-training our people and Nissan Motor Manufacturing Corporation USA had set aside US$56 million for training, including the construction of its training centre. Before production began, we took altogether 420 newly hired managers and technicians in small groups to our plants in Japan for four to six weeks training, as well as introduction to the Japanese way of life. With the combination of the best of the two worlds, meaning the US and Japanese management philosophies, and through what Marvin Runyon, the President, calles the 'participative management' system, the company is now able to produce the best quality trucks and cars in all the USA. Fortune magazine recently selected our US manufacturing company as one of the ten best managed companies in the USA, and we were very pleased with this distinction.

Fifth, we have just completed a US$35 million European Parts Centre in Amsterdam. We will make further efforts to buy European parts and components, both for original equipment and the aftermarket.

Sixth, we announced on 30 January 1981 that we would undertake feasibility studies with an eye towards investing in the UK to manufacture cars. After three years of indecision, Mr Ishihara came to London on 1 February 1984 to sign a memorandum of understanding with Norman Tebbit of the Department of Trade and Industry and to hold a joint press conference. Our game plan is to do it in two steps. In the first stage we will build a pilot plant, employ 400 to 500 people, and assemble 24,000 cars a year. In the second stage we will go into manufacturing 100,000 cars a year with the initial local content of 60 per cent, eventually 80 per cent, some of which will be exported to other EC countries. In the second stage, employment is expected to reach 2,700 and Her Majesty's Government is expected to provide selective financial assistance which is not to exceed £35 million or 10 per cent of the investment. There is no denying that Mrs Thatcher has been a great influence behind this project, inviting us to come here 'to show our example of efficiency'.

As we did in the case of our US investment project, we have taken newly hired managers, senior engineers, supervisors and team leaders in small groups for training in our own plants in Japan.

The Daily Mail dated 15 May 1985 had this to say: 'Japan's new British missionnaries - they'll come home to spread a gospel of loyalty and devotion to the job'.

Tim Torman, 30, who joined Nissan from Talbot, Coventry, said in amazement, 'They are always looking for better ways of doing things. Ordinary people like us are ready to analyse themselves for improvement. The British shy away from change. Here it is on-going.

Steve Milner, 32, formerly a foreman at a frozen food factory, said, 'One big difference you immediately notice in Japan is that they respect people who make things. In Britain people look down on you if you work in a factory'.

Austin-Rover ex-foreman Bill Scott, 37, declared, 'We are determined to build the highest quality cars in Europe. We are going to achieve that target'.

Earlier in the year we advertised for manufacturing staff and as many as 11,000 applied.

In April 1985 Nissan Motor Manufacturing (UK) signed a single union agreement with the AUEW which is unprecedented in the British motor industry.

The new factory buildings for Phase I have just been completed by McAlpines on an 800-acre site in Sunderland, near Newcastle and the first assembled car is expected to come off the assembly line in August 1986.

On site there is what our people there call the 'Liger Spirit'. The Liger is a cross between the Lion of Britain, symbolising strength and justice, and the Tiger of the Orient symbolising dynamism and force.

Now that we have committed ourselves to this project, we want to make a success of it.

Bob Lutz, Chairman of Ford of Europe, has often criticised Japanese car manufacturers for having 'exported unemployment' to Europe.

Nissan is now feeling growing pains in becoming more international and multinational. We do want to be a much larger part of the local scene and want to be able to contribute to the growth of the local economy by providing employment opportunities and by procuring locally produced parts and components. We do also want to be better corporate citizens in whatever country we do our business.

THE COMPARATIVE VALUES OF BRITISH AND JAPANESE MANAGERS

Ritsuko Miyajima
University of Manchester Institute of Science & Technology

Overview
This paper gives a brief account of the findings from continuing research on the comparative values of Japanese and British managers.

The study consists of two phases, the first of which was based on interviews and the second on questionnaires.

The results from the first phase suggest that the Japanese and British managers are different in some of their values in terms of 'Groupism vs. Individualism' and 'Affectivity vs. Neutrality' dimensions.

The second phase of the study largely confirms these differences and, to use TA (Transactional Analysis) terms, the Japanese ideal reminds one of an 'energetic child' and the British of a 'competent adult'.

In addition, the second phase of the study revealed some important differences in the meanings of some of the organisation-related concepts. 'Hardship' is considerably more acceptable to the Japanese but 'individuality' leaves them rather non-commital. The Japanese are less tolerant of 'power' but more lenient towards 'autocrat' then their British counterparts.

This is a half-way report of the findings from a two-phased study on comparative value systems as between British and Japanese managers. Although there are numerous definitions of values, for the purpose of this study, the researcher has taken Rokeach's view which suggested that values are 'abstract ideals, positive or negative, not tied to any specific object or situation, representing a person's beliefs about modes of conduct and ideal terminal modes'(1). In addition, values in this study were regarded to be located in ranking order to form the basis of preferential behaviour.

The first phase

The first phase of the study consisted of 25 interviews (12 Japanese and 13 British managers) in various Japanese subsidiaries within the UK. The purpose of this phase of the study was to explore various 'ideals' in the organisation and to see how different or similar the two groups of managers see each other. Five main issues in these interviews were: an ideal manager, an admired person, an ideal subordinate, aims of work and perceived differences between the Japanese and British manager.

On the issue of 'an ideal manager', both groups agreed on the first criterion which is knowledge, competence and experience to carry out the job. The Japanese, as a second important qualification, chose the ability to communicate with staff and to unite them into a cohesive working group. The British managers' idea of a good manager, on the other hand, was someone who can do the job, can lead, organise, control and utilise his staff. Those different emphases seem to confirm generally believed orientations towards teamwork (groupism) - Japanese, and leading from the front - British.

As a related issue, the respondents were asked to describe the most admired person throughout their organisational life and the two groups again shared the most important characteristics. They admired someone who was able to motivate his staff and able to talk to them. The British managers repeated the importance of the knowledge, competence and experience to carry out the job which he was supposed to do. They also claimed that the persons they admired were not emotional and kept their personal problems outside the office. The Japanese, on the other hand, seemed to consider a person-as-a-whole. They admired someone with his own views and convictions and someone with a 'big stomach'. Someone who can trust his subordinates enough to give a complete free hand in performing a task was mentioned in this vein. The overall pictures conjured up were 'a cool professional' for the British and 'a benevolent father' for the Japanese.

As to the ideal subordinate, similar qualities were also expected by the British and Japanese managers; notably the ability to get on with others and adaptability. The third desired by the two groups was fundamentally the same - interest in work. However, a subtle different was observed in the terms used by the groups. The Japanese managers used the terms 'initiative' (sekkyokusei) and 'enthusiasm' (netsui) more often, while the British described it as 'interest over and above the specified work' and 'willingness'. This difference seemed to suggest that the Japanese managers asked for active involvement and the British for maintenance of smooth operations.

The respondents were than asked to comment how different they saw the other group from themselves. First reported here was the British perception of Japanese managers. The British managers saw the Japanese managers, above all, as group-oriented. This was manifested in various ways in the organisation. The Japanese did not only make decisions based on meetings but were very close to each other outside the company. They were also very keen to keep the 'harmony' of the group and consequently to avoid confrontation. Their strict observance of hierarchy was also noted by some:

> Some of the worst mistakes you can make are to fail to observe the right attitude toward somebody.

There was some disssatisfaction on the part of the British managers regarding this. Some of them felt that the excessive tendency of the Japanese managers towards groupism sometimes excluded the local staff. It is of particular concern, as the longer serving and the more senior British members tended to express this view. The Japanese managers, on the other hand, viewed their British colleagues as individualistic. The British managers were thought to put priority on developing their own careers before the company, and to value their own time very highly. They were also considered very assertive; sometimes to the point of being defensive.

The Japanese also felt that the British managers often possessed an authoritarian attitude and tended to make decisions without so much consultation. The chain of command was very important to them and some Japanese described the distress that they had encountered when this was missed out. They were thought to be rather conservative, preferring the status quo, and to care little for their subordinates.

The last issue in the interview was the aims of work and it was on this topic that the two groups were most apart. Apart from a stable income, the Japanese often expressed rather 'spiritual' aims such as self-actualisation, the purpose of life (ikigai):

> I think I'm trying to find the meaning of life through work.

The British managers sought 'job-satisfaction', which could be described as 'the feeling of one's capability being fully stretched'.

To sum up the findings from this phase of the study, it would be useful to describe the differences between the two groups of managers in terms of two dimensions.

The first dimension is that of 'groupism vs. individualism', on which the Japanese are placed at the groupism end, as opposed to the British being placed at the individualism end.

Groupism such as that displayed by the Japanese managers has various implications for the organisation. It will put priority on achieving group objectives and is likely to consider relationships at work as long lasting ones; as well as to regard colleagues in terms of the 'person-as-a-whole' rather than in terms of their roles. On the other hand, for the individualistic British, work is a means of developing one's career or of supporting a comfortable life-style: the company is the place which provides these opportunities and relationships at work are seen as professional ones based on roles.

The second dimension is to do with 'subjectivity vs. objectivity' or 'affectivity vs. neutrality'. As already seen, the Japanese managers preferred to bring more 'personality' or 'emotional-spiritual' aspects into the workplace. This dimension is perhaps not unrelated to the first one in that the articulation and specification of objectives may be unnecessary in a very cohesive group and in that continual emotional and moral support and exchange for each other may become essential.

The second phase

The second phase of the study was based on questionnaires which were designed with the nature of values and the findings from the first phase in mind. The questionnaire comprises two parts. The first part is composed of 5 sets of values, which respondents were asked to rank order in terms of importance to them. The second part explores the meanings of 10 words on semantic differential scales of 7 gradings.

The questionnaires were distributed to various types of managers both in Japan and the UK. The satisfactory questionnaires out of these returned at this stage were 130 Japanese and 73 British and their breakdown is as follows:

JJJ	(Japanese Managers in Japanese firms in Japan)	40
JJB	(Japanese Managers in Japanese firms in Britain)	29
JBJ	(Japanese Managrs in British firms in Japan)	23
JJJS	(Japanese Managers in smaller Japanese firms in Japan)	38
BBJ	(British Managers in British firms in Japan)	21
BJB	(British Managers in Japanese firms in Britain)	22
BBB	(British Managers in British firms in Britain)	29

This phase of the study was carried out in order to test the hypotheses which arose from the first phase, namely that:

1. There are significant differences in values held by British and Japanese managers.
2. An exposure to a different value system influences the original value system.

Results

The first list of 16 values (List A) is designed to find the more important qualities of an ideal manager and the mean ranking order for each group is listed in Table 1 below for the first 5 and the last 5 values.

The combined results for all the Japanese managers (excepting JJJS, as this group has not yet been matched by the British) and for all the British managers are as follows:

	Japanese combined		British combined
1.	Ability to control	1.	High prof. expertise
2.	Ability to coordinate	2.	Ability to control
3.	Dynamic personality	3.	Ability to coordinate
4.	Flexibility and adaptability	4.	High standards
5.	High professional expertise	5.	Flexibility & adaptabilty
12.	Warmth and sympathy	12.	Knowledge of dept.
13.	Knowledge of department	13.	Patience
14.	A sense of protection	14.	Comradeship
15.	Broadmindedness	15.	Impartial appl. of rules
16.	Patience	16.	Broadmindedness

On the one hand, there are striking similarities in the ways in which the two groups rank-ordered these items, on the other hand, there are a few important differences. The Japanese ranked 'dynamic personality' in third place while it did not appear in the first 5 values chosen by the British. The British, on the other hand, valued 'high professional expertise' and 'high standards of work' more highly than the Japanese.

The second list of 13 items (List B) deals with 'an ideal subordinate'. Table 2 shows the first 4 of the rank-order made by each group.

The combined results for List B are as follows:

Japanese combined		British combined	
1.	Initiative	1.	Initiative
2.	Enthusiasm	2.	Adaptability
3.	A sense of responsibility	3.	Enthusiasm
4.	Originality	4.	A sense of cooperation
10.	Self-confidence	10.	A questioning mind
11.	Calm personality	11.	Calm personality
12.	Respect for the system	12.	A pride in the company
13.	A pride in the company	13.	Respect for the system

'A sense of responsibility' and 'originality' were ranked highly by the Japanese while the British chose 'adaptability' and 'a sense of cooperation'. An interesting dimension amongst the low ranked items was that the Japanese valued self-confidence rather low in their subordinates which may reflect the groupish orientation yet again.

The rank order of List C for each group is shown in Table 3 and the combined results for Japanese and British are as follows:

Japanese combined		British combined	
1.	Self-actualisation	1.	Challenge and stimulation
2.	Satisfaction and fulfilment	2.	Satisfaction and fulfilment
3.	Challenge and stimulation	3.	Standard of living
4.	Standard of living	4.	Prestige and promotion
5.	Prestige and promotion	5.	Belonging
6.	Company	6.	Self-actualisation
7.	Belonging	7.	Company

An important difference here is in the ways in which 'self-actualisation' is ranked by the Japanese and the British managers, which confirms the findings from the first phase of the study. By placing self-actualisation first, the Japanese managers seem to be aiming at more than work or the company can intrinsically provide - perhaps the purpose of life (ikigai).

The fourth list (List D) deals with general life values, and includes Rokeach's terminal values and the rank order for each group is shown in Table 4. The combined results for the Japanese and British for the first 6 and the last 6 values are:

Japanese combined		British combined	
1.	Family security	1.	Family security
2.	Happiness	2.	Happiness
3.	Freedom	3.	Self respect
4.	Sense of accomplishment	4.	Freedom
5.	A comfortable life	5.	A sense of accomplishment
6.	A world at peace	6.	An exciting life
13.	Social recognition	13.	Social recognition
14.	National security	14.	Pleasure
15.	A world of beauty	15.	Equality
16.	Pleasure	16.	A world of beauty
17.	An exciting life	17.	National security
18.	Salvation	18.	Salvation

Amongst the items valued highly, 'a comfortable life' and 'a world at peace' are unique to the Japanese, on the other hand 'self respect' and 'an exciting life' are unique to the British. 'An exciting life' in particular was valued low by the Japanese.

Both 'an exciting life' and 'self-respect' are perhaps the values of individualistic orientation.

The fifth list (List E) is of Rokeach's instrumental values and the rank order for each group is provided in Table 5. The combined results for the Japanese and the British for the first 6 and the last 6 values are as follows:

Japanese combined		British combined	
1.	Responsible	1.	Honest
2.	Broadminded	2.	Responsible
3.	Capable	3.	Capable
4.	Honest	4.	Ambitious
5.	Courageous	5.	Independent
6.	Intellectual	6.	Logical
13.	Forgiving	13.	Cheerful
14.	Ambitious	14.	Polite
15.	Clean	15.	Loving
16.	Polite	16.	Forgiving
17.	Helpful	17.	Clean
18.	Obedient	18.	Obedient

Amongst the first 6 items, the Japanese included 'broadmindedness', 'courageous' and 'intellectual', as opposed to 'ambitious', 'independent' and 'logical' chosen by the British. The items 'ambitious' and 'independent' can be seen as values which are related to 'individualism', and 'ambitious' in particular was ranked very low by the Japanese managers.

The value 'broadmindedness' also calls for further scrutiny as this was ranked low earlier by the Japanese as a quality of 'an ideal manager'. Therefore it suggests that the Japanese managers value this quality in a person in general but not in a manager.

To summarise this part of the second phase, it can be said that overall there is a high degree of agreement across the groups of managers in ranking their ideals. However, several important differences were seen between the Japanese and the British managers.

The differences tended to confirm the dichotomies which were raised by the findings from the first phase of the study and can again be explained by using the dimension 'groupism' vs. 'individualism', and to a lesser degree 'affectivity' vs. 'neutrality'.

To use TA terms, the general impressions of the two managers (the Japanese and the British) are those of an 'energetic child' and of a 'competent adult' respectively as their ideals.

As for the groups which were exposed to the other culture, apparent diversions were noted (see the tables); although whether they were due to the influences of the different value systems or whether people with originally similar values come to work together is a question which awaits further research. But it seems salient to point out that similar values will work better together.

The second part of the questionnaire explores the meanings of 10 organisation-related concepts, (autocrat, change, conflict, democrat, Japanese manager, hardship, individuality, British manager, leadership and power) but in this report, only the ratings from JJJ and BBB are compared, due to limited time and space. The detailed analyses have not been completed at this stage, therefore the comparisons are on the mean figures only. All the concepts are rated in terms of 12 bi-polar objectives.

The term 'autocrat' is rated similarly by the two groups except in two points. The first is that the Japanese rated this concept as little more pleasant than neutral and the British as very unpleasant. The Japanese secondly, saw it as considerably emotional while the British thought it unemotional. The Japanese tolerance of an autocrat can be compared with the British image of 'a cold dictator'.

'Change' was rated almost identically by the two groups and so was the third term 'conflict', except that the British felt the latter concept was stronger and more active than the Japanese did.

The fourth term is 'democrat' and the two profiles are again very similar to each other. An interesting diversion to note is, however, that the Japanese saw the concept as unemotional rather than emotional and the British vice versa.

The next concept, 'British manager', proved to be a rather difficult one for those Japanese who had never experienced working with them; therefore their perception tended to be neutral. The same difficulty applies to the concept of 'Japanese manager' when rated by the British. However, the British managers seemed to be equipped with enough information about the Japanese and they managed to rate it quite closely to the image the Japanese have of themselves. The only notable differences are that the British perceived the Japanese as more unemotional and rational than the Japanese did themselves.

The term 'hardship' provided great variation in perception between the groups. The two profiles of the concept were almost the reverse of each other and while the British saw it as 'bad', 'very unpleasant' 'cold' 'emotional and 'irrational', the Japanese perception of the concept was 'good', 'successful' and 'right'.

The implication here is that the Japanese seem to think that some hardships are necessary in order to succeed. In assessing 'individuality' also, some differences are noted. However, the differences here seem mainly due to the Japanese ambivalence towards the concept; therefore the mean ratings are around the neutral point.

The concept leadership received almost identical ratings from the two groups, as basically good, active, strong, important, successful and right. Not surprisingly perhaps, the profiles of the concept were quite similar to those of 'democrat'.

The ratings for 'leadership' were at the more extreme end for both groups.

The last concept was 'power' and although the profiles are not unlike each other, the Japanese rated it less favourably - in almost every respect. Again the profiles of this concept given by the two groups are quite similar to those of 'autocrat' but the Japanese perceptions of the two concepts are somewhat closer to each other than the British ones. Comparing the four concepts, it is interesting to note that the Japanese were more tolerant of 'autocrat' and the British of 'power'. Although the analysis is as yet incomplete, it seems certain that there are some variations in the meanings of some of the concepts, and a few of them are perhaps very important ones. For example, 'autocrat' was better tolerated by the Japanese than the British partly because the ideal manager/leader in the Japanese mind was close to a 'father figure'. 'Hardship' was a good thing according to the Japanese and this can be the result of the feudal values of frugality and perseverance. This idea of perseverance bringing success in the end probably also explains why the Japanese do not value highly 'ambitiousness' as such.

Although it awaits detailed analysis, the tendency of the Japanese to relate 'emotionality' to 'badness' was noted. It could be considered that the built-in emotionality of the Japanese operates to check its over-expression.

The areas which enfold cultures, values, or attitudes are complicated ones. To some people they are over-subjective and vague and therefore not worth while investigating; but however subjective or vague values may be, the findings from this study suggest that there are some differences between different cultures and that they do matter. It is perhaps important, for example, for a Briton who is going to work for a Japanese organisation to understand that the Japanese management will expect him to go through a certain amount of 'hardship' before he is appraised.

Note

(1) M. Rokeach The nature of human values. The Free Press, New York, 1983.

Table 1

	JJJ		JJB		JBJ		BBJ
1.	Ability to coordinate	1.	Ability to control	1.	Ability to control	1.	Ability to control
2.	Ability to control	2.	Ability to coordinate	2.	Ability to coordinate	2.	Ability to coordinate
3.	Dyamic personality	3.	High moral standards	3.	Dynamic personality	3.	High prof. expertise
4.	Flexibility & adaptability	4.	High prof. expertise	4.	High prof. expertise	4.	High standards
5.	A concern for sub's develop	5.	Dynamic personality	5.	Flex. & adaptability	5.	Dynamic personality
12.	Knowledge of dept.	12.	Comradeship	12.	Comradeship	12.	Patience
13.	Warmth & sympathy	13.	Knowledge of dept.	13.	Warmth & sympathy	13.	Comradeship
14.	Broadmindedness	14.	A sense of protection	14.	Knowledge of dept.	14.	Broadmindedness
15.	A sense of protection	15.	Broadmindedness	15.	Broadmindedness	15.	Knowledge of dept.
16.	Patience	16.	Patience	16.	Patience	16.	Impartial appl. of rule

	BJB		BBB		JJJS
1.	High prof. expertise	1.	High prof. expertise	1.	Ability to control
2.	Ability to control	2.	Ability to coordinate	2.	Ability to coordinate
3.	Ability to coordinate	3.	Ability to control	3.	High moral standards
4.	High standards	4.	High standards	4.	Dynamic personality
5.	Flex. & adaptability	5.	A concern for sub's develop.	5.	High prof. expertise
12.	Trust in subordinates	12.	Patience	12.	Comradeship
13.	Impartial appl. of rules	13.	Knowledge of dept.	13.	Warmth & sympathy
14.	Patience	14.	Impartial appl. of rules	14.	A sense of protection
15.	Comradeship	15.	Comradeship	15.	Broadmindedness
16.	Broadmindedness	16.	Broadmindedness	16.	Patience

Table 2

	JJJ		JJB		JBJ		BBJ
1.	Initiative	1.	Initiative	1.	Initiative	1.	Initiative 2.Enthusiasm2.A sense of responsibility2.A sense of responsibility2.Enthusiasm
3.	Originality	3.	Enthusiasm	3.	Enthusiasm	3.	Adaptability
4.	A sense of responsibility	4.	Originality	4.	A sense of cooperation	4.	Originality
10.	Calm personality	10.	Calm personality	10.	Self-confidence	10.	A questioning mind
11.	Respect for system	11.	Self-confidence	11.	Pride in company	11.	A pride in company
12.	Self-confidence	12.	Respect for system	12.	Respect for system	12.	Calm personality
13.	A pride in company	13.	A pride in company	13.	Calm personality	13.	Respect for system

	BJB		BBB		JJJS
1.	Initiative	1.	Initiative	1.	A sense of responsibility
2.	Adaptability	2.	Adaptability	2.	Initiative
3.	A sense of cooperation	3.	A sense of cooperation	3.	Originality
4.	A sense of responsibility	4.	Enthusiasm	4.	Enthusiasm
10.	A pride in company	10.	Directness	10.	Directness
11.	Calm personality	11.	Calm personality	11.	A questioning mind
12.	Directness	12.	A price in company	12.	Adaptability
13.	A questioning mind	13.	Respect for system	13.	Self-confidence

Table 3

	JJJ		JJB		JBJ		BBJ
1.	Self actualisation	1.	Satisfaction & fulfilment	1.	Challenge & stimulation	1.	Satisfaction & fulfilment
2.	Satisfaction & fulfilment	2.	Challenge & stimulation	2.	Self actualisation	2.	Challenge & stimulation
3.	Challenge & stimulation	3.	Self actualisation	3.	Satisfaction & fulfilment	3.	Standard of living
4.	Standard of living	4.	Standard of living	4.	Standard of living	4.	Prestige & promotion
5.	Prestige & promotion	5.	Prestige & promotion	5.	Prestige & promotion	5.	Belonging
6.	Company	6.	Company	6.	Belonging	6.	Self-actualisation
7.	Belonging	7.	Belonging	7.	Company	7.	Company

	BJB		BBB		JJJS
1.	Challenge & stimulation	1.	Satisfaction & fulfilment	1.	Self actualisation
2.	Satisfaction & fulfilment	2.	Challenge & stimulation	2.	Satisfaction & fulfilment
3.	Standard of living	3.	Standard of living	3.	Challenge & stimulation
4.	Prestige & promotion	4.	Prestige & promotion	4.	Standard of living
5.	Self actualisation	5.	Belonging	5.	Company
6.	Belonging	6.	Company	6.	Belonging
7.	Company	7.	Self actualisation	7.	Prestige & promotion

Table 4

	JJJ		JJB		JBJ		BBJ
1.	Family security	1.	Family security	1.	Family security	1.	An exciting life
2.	Freedom	2.	Happiness	2.	A sense of accompl.	2.	Self respect
3.	Happiness	3.	Freedom	3.	Happiness	3.	A sense of accompl.
4.	A comfortable life	4.	A comfortable life	4.	Freedom	4.	Family security
5.	A sense of accompl.	5.	Wisdom	5.	A world at peace	5.	Happiness
6.	A world at peace	6.	A sense of accompl.	6.	A comfortable life	6.	Freedom
13.	National security	13.	Pleasure	13.	National security	13.	A world of peace
14.	Inner harmony	14.	Equality	14.	Social recognition	14.	Social recognition
15.	A world of beauty	15.	A world of beauty	15.	An exciting life	15.	A world of beauty
16.	Pleasure	16.	Social recognition	16.	A world of beauty	16.	Equality
17.	An exciting life	17.	An exciting life	17.	Pleasure	17.	National security
18.	Salvation	18.	Salvation	18.	Salvation	18.	Salvation

	BJB		BBB		JJJS
1.	Family security	1.	Family security	1.	A world at peace
2.	Freedom	2.	Happiness	2.	Family security
3.	Happiness	3.	Self respect	3.	Happiness
4.	Self respect	4.	Freedom	4.	True friendship
5.	A sense of accompl.	5.	A sense of accompl.	5.	Freedom
6.	An exciting life	6.	An exciting life	6.	National security
13.	Social recognition	13.	Social recognition	13.	Social recognition
14.	Pleasure	14.	A world of beauty	14.	Mature love
15.	Equality	15.	Pleasure	15.	Inner harmony
16.	National security	16.	Equality	16.	Pleasure
17.	A world of beauty	17.	National security	17.	Salvation
18.	Salvation	18.	Salvation	18.	An exciting life

Table 5

	JJJ		JJB		JBJ		BBJ
1.	Responsible	1.	Responsible	1.	Responsible	1.	Responsible
2.	Broadminded	2.	Broadminded	2.	Honest	2.	Capable
3.	Capable	3.	Honest	3.	Broadminded	3.	Honest
4.	Intellectual	4.	Capable	4.	Courageous	4.	Broadminded
5.	Honest	5.	Self-controlled	5.	Capable	5.	Courageous
6.	Courageous	6.	Intellectual	6.	Self-controlled	6.	Independent
13.	Ambitious	13.	Logical	13.	Forgiving	13.	Loving
14.	Clean	14.	Clean	14.	Ambitious	14.	Helpful
15.	Polite	15.	Ambitious	15.	Helpful	15.	Polite
16.	Forgiving	16.	Polite	16.	Clean	16.	Intellectual
17.	Helpful	17.	Helpful	17.	Polite	17.	Clean
18.	Obedient	18.	Obedient	18.	Obedient	18.	Obedient

	BJB		BBB		JJJS
1.	Honest	1.	Honest	1.	Honest
2.	Capable	2.	Responsible	2.	Responsible
3.	Responsible	3.	Capable	3.	Broadminded
4.	Ambitious	4.	Ambitious	4.	Courageous
5.	Logical	5.	Independent	5.	Loving
6.	Polite	6.	Logical	6.	Capable
13.	Clean	13.	Cheerful	13.	Polite
14.	Forgiving	14.	Loving	14.	Logical
15.	Imaginative	15.	Polite	15.	Cheerful
16.	Self-controlled	16.	Forgiving	16.	Ambitious
17.	Loving	17.	Clean	17.	Clean
18.	Obedient	18.	Obedient	18.	Obedient

THE COMMUNICATION STRUCTURE BETWEEN MANAGEMENT AND SHOP FLOOR: A COMPARISON OF A JAPANESE AND A GERMAN PLANT

Ulrich Jürgens and Hans-Peter Strömel
Science Centre, Berlin. Volkswagen AG

The lack of, or the distorted character of, communication between management and shop floor is currently a much debated issue in the auto industries of most Western countries. Since many studies of 'the Japanese success' mention communication as one important factor explaining the loyalty and commitment of Japanese workers, there is a push to alter communication patterns in Western industries and 'learn from the Japanese'.

Indeed, there are quite a lot of studies on, for instance, the institutional setting of labour management consultation in Japanese plants, the Ringi-system, Quality Circles, the many symbols of the 'personal touch' like common lunch rooms, recreation facilities etc.(1). But we are not aware of many case studies of what difference these things really make in handling the day-to-day information processes or problems between management and the shop floor of Japanese plants as compared to Western plants regarding work and manpower-related issues. What are the patterns of structures of communication? Who communicates with whom to settle concerns and grievances? Who becomes informed and involved? What is the relationship between formal and informal structures? What is the relationship between the management hierarchy and the union hierarchy, both of which are, at times conflictually, decision-making and communication structures?

The background research for our upcoming remarks stems from interviews with management and union representatives in two Japanese companies and several Germany companies. Here, however, we are comparing the shop floor process of two cases - one Japanese and one German plant. The processes examined here come from evidence gathered in the body shop and the assembly shop (trim and final assembly) of the plants. We caution that the plants we have chosen to discuss are of very different size and should not be regarded as representative of the national industry in every aspect. However, they do show the differences which we think are 'typical' when comparing German and Japanese plants.

In the following we will first describe the formal structure of the management hierarchy and then the union works council interest representative structure in Japanese and German plants. Secondly, we want to look at the patterns of communication regarding typical processes of handling standard manpower issues in the day-to-day practice in these plants. In the final section, we will draw some conclusions from our findings.

Table 1 shows the supervisory structure in the Japanese and the German plant (for a more detailed breakdown of management positions, the number of rank and file workers and the span of control in the German and Japanese cases, see Appendix A). Let us now take a closer look at the formal task descriptions of the various supervisory levels in our Japanese and German cases. Going from the bottom upwards, we start with the Japanese team-leader (this is the common translation of 'hancho', a translation which is -like some others - quite misleading). The task of the team-leader in direct production in Japan is, according to our interviews, to take care that the work processes in his group (team) go smoothly as a whole. He is expected to be the advisor to his group on personal and technical matters, to carry out the on-the-job training and to serve as a relief man if necessary. He also performs normal production work. In most cases, the team-leader also leads the Quality Circle. In his job description, which is printed on a small card, and which he is required always to carry with him to remind him of his duties, he is admonished to be a shining example to his group in his work behaviour and also in his behaviour as a company employee in public.

The control ratio is one team-leader to six workers; other reports indicate that in other companies this ratio is even lower. Normally, one foreman's group consists of three of these teams. The team is not self-regulating in the sense of the team concept in the debate on new production concepts and job redesign in the West. Rather, work allocation and labour deployment are regulated at the foreman-group level.

In the German case, there is no team-leader in direct production although there is an equivalent, the 'Gruppenleiter', in the machine department. Before going up the hierarchy to foreman, we would like to say a few words about the position of assistant foremen in Japan.

He (always he in Japan) is an assistant and advisor to the foreman, his deputy in case of absences, and keeps a special eye on areas the foreman cannot control. His job description card says:

'The assistant foreman is like the mother in the family. Production control, quality control, safety control, cost control, good cooperation in the work-place and good human relations depend on the extent to which he fulfills his role. As the backbone of the employees of the company, he has to take responsibility and strictly look after the smooth slow of production'. In the German plant, there is no position corresponding to assistant foreman.

In Japan the foreman is clearly the most important person in day-to-day production and manpower deployment. This holds true for the formal description (on his card) as well as the actual situation (based on our interviews). The role of the foreman, as defined on the job description card that he must carry at all times to remind him of his duties, is:

> The foreman has the important duty of guiding the workers and seeing to safety at the work-place, the smooth flow of production and improving productivity. It is above all his duty to put the aims, principles and plans of management into practice. **That means, only through the foreman is the will of the company realised.** The work-place is the place where net value is created. That means that all net value stemming from the transformation of production factors into concrete goods and products is produced under the control and direction of the foreman ... The foreman is the pivotal point at the work-place.

In our interviews with various management representatives of personnel, staff, and production departments, the foreman was called 'almighty' in various instances. He is in charge of manpower allocation, the balancing of the line, the selections for transfers, and, in most instances, he disseminates information to the shop floor, often via the team-leader. He has the position notwithstanding the fact that his superiors have to sign off for final decisions. His span of control is 1:18(17). It is worthwhile noting that the admonitions on the job description card of the foreman in Japan encourage a human relations style of leadership. The following translation illustrates this quite clearly:

> It is up to the foreman to mobilise the workers' energies to achieve company goals. The foreman who can draw the energies out of the workers often says: We (the foremen) want to greet people with a loud voice when we meet them. We want to call the workers by their own names at least once

a day. When we watch the flow of work we want to praise good things and immediately check violations of the rules. We want to eat together with the workers in the lunch-room. We want to systematically try to talk to every worker enough. We want to be sensitive to any change in the workers' behaviour. We want to take immediate note of problems in the workers' private lives. The deep interest in the individual is the source of trust. We want to be good listeners. We want to react to repeated violations of the rules with determination and clear instructions. We have subjects for conversation if we know the following about the individual: Date of birth, date of entrance in the company, internal personal record, rank, basic salary, performance, address, telephone number, transportation use (on the way to work), route taken to the work-place, licences and qualifications, level of skill, training history inside and outside the company, hobbies, character, family structures (name, age), medical history, injuries, vacation record, health limitations to normal performance, number of improvement suggestions made, etc.

In the German plant, the Vizemeister is the first level in the management hierarchy. He is not really the equivalent of the Japanese foreman as he is bound closely to the Meister. One Meister normally has two Vizemeister and it is up to him to divide his territory between them and to delegate jobs for which the Meister still carries ultimate responsibility. In case something must be decided, it is the Meister who must sign off. The Vizemeister would be the first person whom workers from the shop floor would approach to address concerns or problems, whereas the Meister is the initial contact for staff people and others up in the hierarchy concerning shop floor matters. On the average the Vizemeister's span of control is 1 to 37 in the body shop and 1 to 49 in assembly, with a variance of 1 to 24 (in a mechanised area) and 1 to 94 (in a labour intensive area). We were told the goal is to achieve a span of 1 to 40 in assembly.

General foremen in the Japanese case have a very broad span of control: 1 to 155 in the body shop and 1 to 257 in trim and final assembly, meaning they are in control of 10 foreman groups or more. The deputies are not in charge of their own territory and should be regarded as assistants to the general foreman.

The general foreman has the responsibility of signing off and handles controversial cases which could not be settled in the groups. So 'formally the (general foreman) is important but informally the forman is almighty' (interview).

The German Meister seems to be located somewhere between the foreman and the general foreman in the Japanese case. His span of control is 1 to 78 in the body shop and 1 to 99 in trim and final assembly.

However, his span of control varies considerably, for example, in assembly from 1:52 (in a mechanised area) to 1:177 (labour intensive area). The goal is 1:60 in mechanised areas and 1:80 in labour intensive areas. The Meister is in charge of manpower allocation and the balancing of the line on the basis of work standards which are determined by industrial engineering and agreed to by the works council. He controls attendance, and grants vacations and special days off (in accordance with the personnel department).

The Meister seems to have a position comparable to that of the Japanese foreman. In fact, he is also the one regarded as the pivotal point at the work-place by our interview partners. But in terms of span of control and formal responsibilities, the Meister seems to be closer to the general foreman. It seems more appropriate, therefore, to use different terms and not to translate 'Meister' as 'foreman' or 'general foreman'. A job description card of the duties and responsibilities of the Meister is also distributed. But, in contrast to the human relations focus in the Japanese case, the task description (which has altogether 21 items) reads like the functions of an administrative body.

In fact there are many complaints about the administrative overload in the day-to-day work of the Meister, and that there is no time left for the 'human touch'.

We will not go further up the hierarchy in our analysis because the general foreman level is the last that can really be called shop floor related.

Summarising this section we can do an easy calculation which shows the immense difference between the Japanese and German cases regarding the density of supervision on the shop floor. Taking all levels, including the 'playing leaders' (this is a Japanese term for management personnel without direct supervisory functions), together, the ratio in the Japanese case is 1 to 3, 4 (body), 3,3 (assembly). In the German case, the ratio is 1 to 24,9 (body), and 32,9 (assembly). Thus, the 'density' supervision is 8 to 10 times greater in the Japanese plant. From these cases, we cannot of course generalise the comparison of the density factor for all Japanese and German automobile plants. Due to the enormous size of the plant in the German case, the ratio there seems to be an extreme case.

But even the German average would be far less than the Japanese. (The German average would also be, although to a smaller extent, less than the average of French and English plants)(2).

Obviously this result tells us much about career patterns and human resource development in both cases; but what does it mean in terms of the regulation of day-to-day production and manpower issues?

Before we come to our tentative answers we have to bring one more actor brieftly into play: the union. Looking at the 'span of interest representation', for example, the ratio between workers or shop stewards, the picture seems very similar in both cases (see Table 2). In each plant, there is, on a company average, one union representative for every twenty workers. This means three to four union shop stewards for one Meister in the German case, and one shop steward to one group leader in the Japanese case. The next step in the German case would be the works council members who are responsible for production areas (Bereichsbetriebsträte). They have a span of interest representation of 1 to 1,200 or 1,500 and represent more or less at the level of departments. There are also coordinators for the four main production areas of the plant. At the plant level, there is the works council and its executive committee. In the Japanese case, there are one or two directors of the union at the plant level. Quite clearly there is a discrepancy between German and Japanese representation beyond the shop steward level but this is compensated for somewhat by the fact that the German works council members do not have work obligations, whereas in the Japanese plan only the one or two directors are able to devote themselves full-time to union affairs.

Another important difference is in the relationship between supervisors and union representatives. In both cases supervisors can theoretically be union representatives at the same time. But whereas in the German case only a handful out of a hundred Vizemeister (and the same for the Meister) are shop stewards, the identity of a union role and management role in one person is quite common in the Japanese case. And, whereas the Meister who are shop stewards represent the interests of other salaried employees, the Japanese foreman who is also a shop steward would represent the interests of the hourly workers in his area. We do not have details for the Japanese case, but it seems that the linkage between the supervisory and union roles is quite pronounced in Japan. The union hierarchy matches the management hierarchy: union districts correspond to management territories. Thus, observers in the industrial relations setting in the Japanese automobile industry see the general foreman as the backbone of the union structure. The combined identity of supervisor and union representative ties together union and management communication channels in a way which explains much of the difference in the communication patterns between the German and the Japanese case.

Communication patterns in the Japanese and the German case

We looked at two types of communication: Communication of upper management decisions down to the shop floor and communication of shop floor concerns etc. to upper management. The situations we selected for examples of downward communication were the scheduling of an extra shift, the scheduling of overtime, and the transfer of personnel. As to upward communication we looked at concerns about work standards, concerns about the work environment, the wish for personal holidays, personal wishes to be sent on special training courses, and the wish to be transferred to another work group, section, etc.

Communicating top level decisions to the shop floor

The scheduling of extra shifts belongs to the type of decisions that are made by the management executive board and which need to be agreed by the top union or works council representatives. Other decisions would be those relating to bonus agreements or early retirement etc. With regard to these decisions there is concern among German managers that the union/works council channel of communication is quicker and more effective in conveying the actual content of the agreement down to the shop floor; and that who informs first becomes regarded as the more competent informant. The consequence is that people on the shop floor, including the Meister, ask the union representatives/works council member and not the management in cases when there are rumours about important central decisions.

In the Japanese case, the management channels down to the foreman are regarded as quicker and more effective. The union president stressed that there is parallel and synchronised information processing down to the shop floor by both the management and the union. The foreman should be the one to give the information to the rank and file and his authority should not be undermined. We should not forget that he is also a union member, so he would be informed about decisions from the centre by both sides. Thus, his double role is very favourable for smooth communication.

There is another line of centrally made decisions that are in the category of the production programme and the scheduling of mix and volume for the next respective planning period. In the Japanese case these programmes are planned on a monthly basis; in the German case, quarter annually, and then weekly. Decisions on, for instance, overtime and transfer of personnel are often consequences of these schedules.

In the Japanese case, there are general agreements on the amount of overtime and the limits to transfers which management can enforce without special consultation. But consultation would take place even in these cases. Let us assume that management wants to schedule more than the agreed 1.75 hours overtime per day shift (0.75 hours for nightshift). For this they would need a previous consultation meeting with the union at the central level. In such cases the union might consult the membership informally and casually (for example, during breaks etc.). But there might not actually be any consultation; it is enough that the union delegates convey their approval. There is no case reported by management when the union has ever failed to approve overtime but this is explained by processes of 'pre-consultation', so that management would not put forward demands in instances where dissaproval could be expected. After the decision is taken the foreman will inform the rank and file workers and they have to regard this as obligatory work duty. Transfers due to the production schedule can also be handled freely between jobs within the section. The union would be concerned only in cases of transfers between plants and permanent transfers between departments. The selection of who goes and who stays, in the case of most transfers within the department, is decided within the groups either by internal rules or by the decision of the foreman.

With respect to production scheduling, the German company follows the principle of producing according to the personnel situation (output varies according to expected attendance levels). Therefore, there will be no general overtime besides jointly agreed extra shifts. Overtime for special groups or overtime resulting from breakdowns, etc. on a short time basis is applied for by the Meister and decided at an ad hoc meeting at the departmental level with the area works council representative (if there are no political or general issues at stake - in such cases it would go to the plant or even company level). The selection of who has to do overtime is decided by the Vizemeister or Meister (the latter in controversial cases). It does sometimes happen that individuals have to be specially 'persuaded', but the result is almost always compliance. Theoretically, individual cases of protest against overtime can be taken up to the level of the department where they would normally be settled between the area works council members and the department head. Management claims it is rare for the decision of the Meister to be overruled by upper level management due to union works council intervention.

With respect to transfers, the picture is similar to Japan. The union/works council member would become involved only in individual transfer cases if these go across departmental lines or if they are likely to last more than a certain period, such as four weeks, which may differ according to cases and areas etc. The selection for transfer is done by the Vizemeister, and in controversial cases by the Meister, and so on.

Upward communication of shop floor concerns

Communication processes resulting from individual complaints about work allocation, work standards, work environment strain etc. seem to follow a formalised pattern in the Japanese case. Joint management/labour consultation committees exist all the way from the company level down to the departmental level. See, for instance, Table 3 which is of another company but seems to be quite similar to our case. Thus, complaints would normally be addressed to the team-leader first, then to the foreman, who in the case of work standards is responsible anyway. Theoretically both management and union representatives can take a problem to the joint committees at the departmental level. However, the combined identity of the union/supervisory role can make it difficult to bring worker concerns into the formalised grievance structure.

Far more important than such formalised structures are the informal ones in Japan. Questions of work environment can be taken up by the Quality Circles at the team-leader's level. Work allocation and work standard complaints are regarded as internal problems of group cooperation, support of the neighbours, support by the team-leader and re-allocation by the group leader. With respect of complaints about work intensity, the union president interviewed declared frankly that the union does not like workers to take the formal official route via the committee but expects problems to be settled informally at the group level. Complaints should be addressed to the foreman. If there were complaints, it would probably be because the worker was sick. In such a case his workload would be reduced and reallocated to somebody in good shape. If there are many complaints in one foreman's area, however, it might be an indicator that he is not a good foreman, and that should show up in his personal assessment.

In the German case, there is quite a low degree of 'going through the proper channels' in dealing with complaints. Instead, professionals are brought in. Work environment complaints, for instance, would probably be taken up to the safety arena and addressed by the safety delegates of the union, the safety representatives of the plant, the company doctor or medical team, etc. Complaints about work standards, if not easily settled by the Vizemeister/Meister, would result in reassessment by industrial engineers. In both cases the shop steward of the area would be present and, according to the general agreement in the company, the result would have to be accepted by him (as the representative of the works council). Afterwards the person who had complained would have to accept the (new) standard, or be transferred, or receive further training. Who would take up the complaint? This is up to the worker: he could go to the shop steward, the works council member for his area, the Vizemeister or the Meister. It varies from case to case, but in general, it goes fifty-fifty through management or union channels.

With regard to the wishes of individual employees to be transferred to other departments or to be transferred to other jobs within the department for broadening job qualifications or to be sent on training courses, in the Japanese case transfers to other production areas would require an application to the personnel department. Before such a step, the individual could talk to the 'management advisor' of the department. In each department an experienced general foreman who was relieved of his supervisory duties at the age of 55, like all lower and middle management supervisors in the company, becomes such an advisor for the last five years until his retirement. Transfer wishes would **not** be addressed to union representatives.

In Japan the main reason for transfers within sections is job rotation, according to our interviews. The selection of people for transfer is done by the foreman. The foreman is required to have, for each of his workers, a plan for multi-skill formation in his area. He will nominate candidates for training courses. The union is not involved in these matters at all. Individual wishes to be nominated or to be sent on training courses without the consent of the foreman would hardly be realistic, and could only occur on a private basis during vacation or in the evening.

In the German case, individual wishes to be transferred to other production areas also require an application to the personnel department. For information, the employee could go to the personnel office in the area (the personnel department has decentralised offices for routine work) or to the area works council members. Transfer wishes within the department would normally be motivated by wage considerations. If somebody wants to be a rectifier in trim and final assembly he would talk to the Vizemeister. The Vizemeister would rotate him to other jobs in the area on a try-out and test basis. If the Vizemeister refuses to comment positively on the transfer wish, the shop steward can be involved and the case can be raised to a higher level. But this seldom happens; most cases are settled at the Vizemeister and Meister level. The task description for the Meister exhorts him among other stipulations, to 'Support employees in the development of their skills (for example, guidance, instruction) and to make suggestions to his superior for advance/training measures.' According to our interviews, the Vizemeister/Meister will think of ways to support their able workers; they might nominate them for training courses and rotate them round different jobs. They also talk informally with the works council members with comments such as 'we want to promote this guy'. The Vizemeister and Meister play the active role in this human resource development: rank and file workers almost never take the initiative in asking for further training.

Individual wishes as to when to take one's vacation or personal holidays etc. to which he is contractually entitled

In the Japanese case, the foreman is responsible for the administration of attendance/absences: in the German case the Meister. There seems to be quite a small potential for problems and conflicts in the Japanese case, and a very great one in the German case. In the Japanese case, interviewees both from management and the union stressed that a scheduled, paid holiday system is promoted both by the company and the union. To promote the actual use of the vacation entitlements, Committees for the Promotion of Use of Vacation Entitlements were set up for each foreman's area. The respective shop stewards for the areas (who could be foremen themselves) administer the vacation calendar for the group. Although the individual entitlement varies between 14 and 20 days, only one fifth was actually used by workers in 1983 in the company discussed in this paper(4). Even if we take into account the few remaining days actually taken off, there seems to be no real problem of scheduling and rescheduling. Assuming a worker wants to change the date of a planned day off and the group leader decides negatively - what would happen? The union president says extra individual wishes should be discussed in the group and problems should be solved there: the union should not be involved at all.

In the German case, the administration of vacation and special vacation entitlements are delegated by the Meister to one of the Vizemeister; the responsibility and the controversial cases are up to the Meister.

In addition to the 15 days shut down vacation period, there is a remaining 15 days of vacation entitlement, 9 days of 'free shifts' according to the new agreement on reduced working time, a yearly average of 2, 5 days of special recreation leave, and 4 days, on an individual average for special education individually. Management claims that they do not try to influence the decision of the individual about whether to use their entitlements for special education or recreational leave. For the shop steward there is clearly an interest in raising the absentee level and thereby creating new employment opportunities.

Decisions on the actual timing of leave are up to the Meister, but it can happen that workers could try to overthrow this decision with the help of the shop steward/works council members who can introduce the worker's position at the level of the department or the production area and obtain another management decision. More often than not, however, the steward or the works council members consult the Meister and then accept his reason. Only in isolated cases is the decision of the Meister turned around in the way described above.

Summary and Conclusions

We want to summarise our findings in four points:

Firstly, there is an immense difference in the 'supervisory density' on the shop floor of the Japanese and the German plants. If one among three to four people crowding the floor has some kind of a management position, management virtually has taken root on the shop floor. The notion of self-regulation on the shop floor under such conditions does not mean a withdrawal of management from the shop floor but rather a diffusion of management onto the shop floor. Although the role of the group as the arena for problem solving and informal conflict solutions is to be stressed for the Japanese case, as expected, the role of the foreman should not be overlooked. The foreman still has classical management tools and powers unrivalled by staff, or professionals, etc. The authority of the foreman has not been eroded by the team. On the contrary, both management and the union agree to support his authority. Thus, even though teams have internal methods of communicating and solving problems, the problems can also be solved just by the authoritative decision of the foreman. There was no sign of a 'Meister-Krise', as it is discussed in many Western countries(5).

Secondly, the Japanese companies often have an impressive, formalised set-up of labour/management consultation, and of committees to settle problems and solve grievances. In practice, however, it is expected that the problems and complaints will be settled informally at the group level. There seems to be a prevalent notion of the group as the family, and solving problems within the family is regarded by the union as beneficial to the individual. Thus, if somebody wants to complain, for instance, about not being promoted, or for getting a negative personal assessment, etc., the union would give him the advice to seek the informal solution because the formal procedure might reveal his identity to the company public and lead to disadvantages for him. In contrast to the formalised Japanese labour/management consulting system, the German institutional set-up is scant, and consultation takes place on a more ad hoc basis.

Thirdly, the role of professionals to solve grievances is much more important in the German case. In many instances of individual complaints, the cases are handed over to these professionals. It seems that, when these professionals come into play they are more concerned about the objective factors, for example, measurement of drag, toxic concentration, time and motions required to do the job. etc. In the Japanese case, industrial engineers would not enter the scene - according to the interview partners - in cases of individual concerns about the workload. But workload or work environment could be topics for the discussion in the team and/or the Quality Circle. In this context the diagnosis of the problem would include subjective perceptions of the individual and social implications of the problem. Then the professional engineers stationed in the section, and who are often part of an 'improvement group' of engineers and skilled workers would be called in(6). In the end, specific proposals for improvement which were generated by the workers themselves might be put into practice through the activities of the improvement groups.

Fourthly, in the German case there are more opportunities for the individual to bring forward his complaints or wishes and these complaints/demands can more easily go up the hierarchy via the union/works council representatives. The workers turn either to the union representatives or management representatives (nearly fifty-fifty) when they bring forward their complaints/demands; the matter might be taken to the general foreman, but it might also be taken to the department directly. In this pluralist situation, it can happen that the decisions of low level supervisors get turned around. In any case, from the perspective of the individual worker, there are more opportunities to present his or her view and achieve what he or she wants. In the Japanese case, the highly intertwined character of union and management positions on the shop floor have the effect that the first level supervisors are almost unassailable. The system seems to work without the safety valves for the dissenting views and demands of the individuals. Maybe the group's function as a family serves as an equivalent.

Finally, it has become evident that formal communication structures like consultation bodes, ringi, etc. are not sufficient means for the improved flow of communication up and down the company ladder. Communication problems, therefore, cannot easily be solved by a transfer of such institutions. In the Japanese context, communication seems to be a smooth process which, as we have shown, relies on the classical hierarchical roles and channels. Themes and motives for communication are dominated by management definitions and management issues. Shop floor groupism seems to take care flexibly and informally of the rest. Communication in Western countries would inevitably be closely linked to questions of interest representation and bargaining. The themes and motives for communication are sometimes expressly against management definitions etc. It seems implausible that communication problems under these conditions can be solved in the Japanese way.

Formal structure of management hierarchy and union representation

Table 1 Shop floor supervisory structure and span of control in the body shop in trim and final assembly of a Japanese and German plant

	Japanese plant	German plant
1: 160	---general foreman 1:155/257(1)	
140		
120		
100		
80	--------------------------------	Meister 1:78/99
60		
40	--------------------------------	Vizemister 1:37/49
20		
	-----foreman 1:17/18	
	-----assistant foreman 1:15/16	
	-----teamleader 1:6/6	

(1) First figures refer to Body Shop, second to Trim and Final Assembly.

Table 2 Union/works council structure in a Japanese and a German plant

	Japanese Company		German Company	
Company Level	Executive Committee	Executive Office	Vorstand	General Works Council
Plant Level	Plant Manager	Union Directors 2-4	Betriebsleiter	
	Division Manager		Bereichsleiter	Works Council 63 (Plant Exec. Committee) 10)
	Division Deputy Man.		Hauptabteilungsleiter	Works Council Members as Coordinators
	Dept. Manager		Abteilungsleiter	
	Section Manager		Unterabteilungsleiter	Works Council Members (with resp. for part. areas)
Shop Floor Level	General Foreman	Delegates (Ø 1:155)	Meister	
			Vizemeister	
	Group Leader	Shop stewards (Ø 1:20)		Shop stewards (Ø 1:20)
	Rank and file		Rank and file	

Table 3: Listening to worker's grievances to improve the working environment

Discerning members' complaints and desires		Negotiation with the company and settlement of problems	
Executive committee	Discussion, investigation and reform-ulation	Joint round-table conference or specialised committee	President and directors
Chief shop stewards	Discussion, investigation, and reform-ulation	Branch/Plant-level round-table conference	Plant, depart-mental, and assistant departmental managers
Councillors and shop stewards	Discussion, investigation, and reform-ulation	Shop-level round-table conference	Departmental, assistant departmental, and section managers

Input from union members

The nature and scope of a suggested improvement or a grievance determines the level at whichit will be taken up for discussion.

Source: Federation of Toyota Workers' Unions(3).

Table 4 Span of controls of supervisors and span of interest representation of shop stewards and works councillors in a Japanese and German plant

Position			Japan Body	Japan Trim & final assembly	FRG Body	FRG Trim & final assembly
Bucho	Abteilungs-leiter	Production manager	?	?	1:821 6	1:2.853 3
Kacho (Section manager)(1)	Unter-Abteilungs-leiter	Superin-tendent	1:309 4	1:593 4	1:260 19	1:1.426 6
Kocho resp. Kakaricho Shunin (fore-man)(1)	Meister	General foreman	1:155 8(8)	1:297 8(14)	1:78 63	1:99 86
Kumicho resp Shokucho (Groupleader)(1)	Vizemister	Foreman	1:18 67(83)	1:17 140(148)	1:37 135	1:49 174
Hancho(2) (Teamleader)(1)	Gruppenleiter	Teamleader	1:6 197	1:6 403	none	none
	Rank and file		1.236	2.373	4.930	8.650
(Shop Committee Officers)(1)	Vertrauensleute	Shop stewards	1:20(3)		1:20(4)	
(Delegates, Councillors)(1)	Bereichsbet-riebsräte	Area works councillors	1:150-200		1:1200-1500	

1) Common translation from Japanese
2) No supervisory role
( ) Number of deputies
3) Average of company
4) Average of plant

Notes

(1) T. Inagami, Labour-Management Communication of Workshop Level, Tokyo, 1983.
S.J. Park, 'Labour-Management Consultation as a Japanese Type of Participation: an International Comparison', in S. Tokunaga and J. Bergmann (eds.), Industrial Relations in Transition. The Cases of Japan and the Federal Republic of Germany, University of Tokyo, 1984.
S.J. Park, Mitbestimmung in Japan. Produktivität durch Konsultation, Campus Verlag, Frankfurt/New York, 1982.
T. Shirai, Contemporary Industrial Relations in Japan, University of Wisconsin, Madison, 1983.
E. Vogel (ed.), Modern Japanese Organisation and Decision-Making, University of California, Berkeley, 1985.

(2) J. Child and B. Partridge, Lost Managers - Supervisors in Industry and Society, Cambridge University Press, 1982. M. Maurice, F. Sellier and J-J Silvestre, 'The Search for a Societal Effect in the Production of Company Hierarchy. A Comparison of France and Germany', in P. Osterman (ed.), Internal Labour Markets, Massachusetts Institute of Technology, Cambridge, Mass., 1984.

(3) Federation of Toyota Workers Unions, Union Activities at Toyota. Basic Concepts, Organisation, Activities, 1984, p.28.

(4) M Nomura, Betriebsgewerkschaften und Arbeiter in Japan, conference paper, Euro-Japanese Management Studies Association Conference, Berlin, 1985.

(5) H. Bargmann, 'Innovationshemmnis Industriemeister?', Zeitschrift für Soziologie, Vol. 13, No.1, pp. 45-59.
Child and Partridge op.cit.

(6) R. E. Cole, Work, Mobility and Participation, University of California, Berkeley, 1980, p.181.

THE INTERNATIONALISATION OF JAPANESE FINANCIAL INSTITUTIONS

A.R. Prindl
Nomura International Ltd.

Internationalisation can take several forms:

Internationalisation of earning streams;
Internationalisation of assets;
Internationalisation of foreign operations;
Internationalisation of shareholders;
Internationalisation of management;

For financial institutions, the first two of these aspects go hand in hand and indeed the Japanese financial houses have increasingly moved into foreign lending over the last two decades. In the latter two areas not much yet can be described. There are only very small foreign shareholders in the Japanese houses (although the recent flurry in Japanese bank stocks may show that this has changed) and there are virtually no cases of Western senior management in those houses to date. However, the internationalisation of Japanese banks' and brokers' foreign operations is proceeding rapidly and will certainly lead over time to stronger, more competitive and more internationalised institutions as a result.

This brief paper takes the Japanese houses and their presence in London as its focus, as symbolic of internationalisation now taking place.

To a large extent, the establishment of Japanese financial entities in Europe has been in the Euro-markets, another factor being to follow Japanese industrial and trading companies settled in the host nation. By far the most important centre of operations has been London, not in itself a new trend, since the Bank of Tokyo, for instance, had a branch there as early as 1881.

Their operations have taken several forms. Most commercial banks are in the form of branches, which eliminate the need for their own capital. Brokerage houses have set up separate broking/merchant banking subsidiaries in London and other

European cities, some of which offer commercial banking services. Taking London as the chief example, Japanese financial houses had the representation in early 1985 shown in Table 1 below.

This is a large number of banks in one market from one country, even given the size and dominance of London. In the banking area particularly, that array of lenders has been chasing a limited number of Japanese borrowers, causing spreads to dwindle to the vanishing point. At times it has been reported that they have received guidance from the Bank of England as to the appropriateness of these spreads (particularly in the Banker's Acceptance market). Japanese lending activity and competitive rates have spilled over to Western borrowers, and the outcome is striking in the UK., where Japanese institutions account for some 23 per cent of all banking assets (see Table 3).

Japanese brokers, whose subsidiaries in Europe at first specialised in selling indigenous stocks and bonds to European investors, have now developed a booming trade in selling European paper back to Japanese takers, and a fast growing underwriting business as well.

Motives for coming

The factors behind the avid movement of Japanese houses to London and other parts of Europe are several, and include both business reasons and structural ones.

Business reasons

(1) Assisting Japanese firms abroad

Japanese commercial banks have emulated other institutions in following their domestic clients abroad. Earlier waves of American banks, then British and Continental European ones, had set up foreign branches in the overseas markets where their main customers were establishing manufacturing and trading subsidiaries, having a relatively certain chance of business. The sharply increasing trend of Japanese direct investment in Europe, buttressing this argument, is shown in Table 2 below.

(2) Maturity of the home market

The interest of Japanese houses in directly working with their biggest domestic customers abroad has been greatly augmented by the need to find new lending outlets. Sometime in the 1970's Japan became a mature economic country. Reconstruction after World War II had been completed and most Japanese industries possessed very modern plants. While social infrastructure left (and still leaves) a great deal to be desired, the banks have seen little chance to lend large amounts in that sector, nor has the high savings rate of the Japanese customer yet allowed a strong retail lending base. Japanese domestic loan demand has consequently fallen in the last half decade, once the dramatic but rapidly overcome effects of the oil shock were over. The urge to offset this shortfall in home demand was an important factor in the decision to increase foreign operations.

(3) Entering fields closed to them in Japan

The Japanese financial system is segmented, with still strict barriers separating types of institutions. Commercial banks are rigidly divided into a dozen city banks (like British clearing banks), one foreign exchange bank (Bank of Tokyo which specialises in foreign transactions), seven domestic trust banks, three long-term credit banks, and many regional or cooperative institutions. All are separated from the brokerage houses by Article 65 of the Japanese Securities Exchange Act, which follows Glass Steagall in prohibiting single institutions from engaging in both lending and underwriting in Japan. This restriction does not apply abroad, and many Japanese banks are becoming underwriters/securities dealers in London or elsewhere.

The most striking example of this was the purchase of majority control of Banca del Gottardo in Lugano by Sumitomo Bank in 1984. This is the first major acquisition by a Japanese financial house of a European one; its cost was reported to be US$144 million. Banca del Gottardo is an important institution in the Swiss bond market and possesses excellent underwriting and distribution capabilities. This aggressive move suits the style and image of Sumitomo, the most profitable commercial bank in Japan and one which has stressed its in-house corporate finance capability in Tokyo. More usual has been the establishment of merchant banking/underwriting subsidiaries in London by virtually all of the major Japanese banks. Typically called Mitsubishi Finance International, Mitsui Finance International, etc., they are beginning to lead security issues for Japanese issuers (not only from their own Keiretsu groupings) or to act as prominent managers and co-managers in issues led by U.S. or European banks.

The Japanese brokerage houses are also diversifying towards commercial banking. To date this has largely taken the form of banking subsidiaries in Amsterdam or Luxembourg, three of which are carrying on securities business as well. These engage in syndicated lending and the interbank market, although at still relatively small volumes. The brokers' desire to create full-scale banking operations in London has been the basis of prolonged discussions between the two Governments as to supervision and reciprocity questions; these continue at the time of writing.

Structural Reasons

(1) To be directly in the biggest market

Japan is far away, with a non-overlapping time zone, and its own capital markets have been traditionally small and tightly regulated. It is attractive not only for immediate competitive reasons to be directly involved in larger markets, but also for longer term structural reasons. Later in the century there will be fewer international financial institutions in the world - maybe 50 large groups - but the dominant ones will be much larger. Those institutions will cover the waterfront of financial services, including both commercial banking and securities business. The leading survivors will have to maintain a major foothold in each of the three world financial centres: London, Tokyo and New York. Putting one's act together in London, still the largest and most open of the three, can be seen as a long range strategic move in preparation for the globalisation and concentration of international finance.

(2) Recycling Japanese capital outflows

Japan has now become the world's largest capital exporter and this trend is likely to continue. The Japanese trade surpluses are running around US$50 billion annually, or the level of Saudi Arabian surpluses at their largest. Slightly more than this amount is presently being repumped out of Japan in direct and portfolio investments. Much of the intermediary function in the purchases of foreign stocks and bonds is carried out by the London (and New York) outlets of the Japanese brokers, which has caused them to rapidly expand their product lines and staff. The underwriting subsidiaries of the Japanese commercial banks also play a role here.

(3) Internationalisation of the Yen

A third factor, greatly in favour of the Japanese houses, is the internationalisation of their own currency. Until very recently, the Japanese yen was not in any sense an international currency. It was not used much in trade invoicing, nor held in international reserves, nor borrowed in large amounts except in the form of Samurai bonds. The latter - domestic yen borrowed by foreign governments - were chiefly used by the Japanese government to offset Balance of Payments inbalances, and did not represent a free market.

Now, the yen has been firmly set out on the road to internationalisation from a variety of endogenous and exogenous forces (especially American pressure). Euro-yen straight bonds for private sector companies were permitted in December 1984, followed by a succession of variants tapping longer term Euro-yen for the first time. Obviously, Japanese houses have the best change to cominate this market. Other aspects of internationalisation - the use of yen in trade and in the composition of international reserves, tapping of private placement sources of yen, and the placement of foreign shares in the Tokyo Stock Market - will likewise bring increased business opportunities to Japanese institutions.

Size

Most Japanese banking operations in London take the form of branches, therefore estimates of their overall business are difficult to obtain. However, the Bank of England publishes aggregate figures of the Japanese banks' assets in London, which are reproduced in Table 3. The striking growth of their assets from 1980 to 1985 and the percentage they now represent of total banking business in England is readily apparent.

The Japanese brokerage houses have achieved a very large turnover reflecting the strong home interest in foreign bonds and stocks. Japanese investors have become among the largest purchasers of these instruments in the London market place.

Staffing

Traditionally, Japanese houses have been very heavily dependent upon expatriates and the median number of Japanese managers in the larger banks and brokerage houses is over 40. The Bank of Tokyo, for example, has come 65 Japanese in its various London operations. Only recently have Westerners begun to play a role in the management of these London offices, but there are a few signs that this is now happening. The Japanese have begun to recruit experienced specialists - especially in dealing and capital markets - from the City and also new graduates from the main British universities.

Nomura International Limited appears to be the furthest along this path. It has nearly 100 professionals who are Westerners, derived from both sources. For example, in 1985 it hired 26 new or recent graduates from Oxbridge and other British universities, all of whom are now in Tokyo undergoing cultural and professional training. The other Japanese houses are beginning to emulate this step as part of their own internationalisation. However, senior management members who are Western are still very limited, and most decisions appear to be made in conjunction with Tokyo, and in the Japanese language.

Competitive implications

The world has seen the phenomenal success of Japanese industry in successive waves of products, moving through textiles, ships and steel, autos, cameras, electronics, ball bearings, etc., and now in the high tech areas. The sizeable capital of Japanese financial institutions, their involvement in the world's second strongest economy, which itself has become a huge capital exporter, and the likelihood that Tokyo will become a major financial market in its own right lead one to believe that Europe will be competing fiercely with the Japanese in financial services in the future. The UK banking statistics bear this out (as do those in America). The capital, balance sheet strength and distribution power of Japanese houses show that they certainly have the strength to compete.

Indeed, until liberalisation of the Japanese domestic financial markets is further along, or local demand there increases, all the factors so far pushing the Japanese into more aggressive financial competition here are likely to continue. Diversification of services in particular would appear to be the key factor, which simply means that Japanese will be noticed in almost every type of financial deal. In any case, they represent huge placing power; in many instances, they will be competing directly for lead mandates. Importantly, they have added to their capital and placement strengths the ability to intermediate and organise swaps, at present the driving force in the international bond markets.

Western reactions

Western competitors are fully aware of these trends, and their reactions have taken a variety of forms. Certain astute ones have forged quiet and informal alliances with friendly Japanese houses, with resulting joint deals or co-lead management positions, or cooperative ventures such as Barclay's move into trust banking in Japan with Toyo Trust as its partner.

Other firms, frustrated by the inability to do more in Japan, have been more belligerent. The commercial banking business of UK and other Western banks' branches in Tokyo has suffered; few are making profits. However W.I. Carr, Warburg and Kleinwort Benson have recently been given securities licenses in Tokyo. Warburg, Vickers da Costa and Jardine Fleming have been allowed to purchase a seat on the Tokyo Stock Exchange.

Reciprocity is often mentioned, even by the Governor of the Bank of England, and sometimes the nastier term **retaliation.** There is a reciprocity clasue in the criteria for new corporate members of the London Stock Exchange, in which access of UK firms to the relevant foreign stockmarket will be a key factor. This could eventually affect Japanese entry into the new gilts market. The Department of Trade and Industry has also put such a clause into the new Financial Services bill which will regulate investment activities in the City.

However, reciprocity and the threat of retaliation are likely to dwindle after the opening of Tokyo. While the Western side builds its own Tokyo base, the importance of comparative advantages of all the major players in world finance will come to the surface. We have not seen fully international structures before; the limitations of networks or markets have not allowed any institution to build the ideal base for long range changes in financial markets. Integration of local staff, both at top levels and in mid management, will be the next concomitant step for the Japanese to take. Given their size, capital, placing power and expertise (or ability to import/learn financial expertise quickly) it lacks only the 'delivery systems' - good local officers to deliver those strengths and market products - for the Japanese to be a very formidable force in international finance. Their effort in London should thus be an extremely interesting example to study.

Table 1 Japanese financial companies in London, early 1985

Direct branches of banks	23
Subsidiaries of banks	14
Representative offices of banks	12
Subsidiaries of brokerage houses	13
Representative offices of brokerage houses	1
Consortium banks and others	3
	66

Source: Euromoney. Annual Survey of Foreign Banks in London, April 1985

Table 2 Japanese direct investment in Europe FY 1977 - FY1984 (US $ million)

FY	1977	220
	1978	323
	1979	495
	1980	578
	1981	798
	1982	876
	1983	990
	1984	1937

Source: JETRO

Table 3 Japanese bank assets in the UK

	Total assets of all banks in UK (A)	Assets of Japanese banks in UK (B)	B/A %
	(£ million)		
Dec. '80	303,279	40,817	13.5
June '81	372,284	57,659	15.5
Dec. '81	424,062	70,171	16.5
June '82	469,048	79,180	16.9
Dec. '82	540,024	99,439	18.4
June '83	567,278	107,463	18.9
Dec. '83	631,552	122,876	19.5
June '84	684,507	140,058	20.5
Dec. '84	759,834	167,602	22.1
May '85	743,668	163,351	22.0
Oct. '85	736,429	169,600	23.0

Source: Bank of England - Quarterly Bulletins

HOW TO ELIMINATE RISK IN RECRUITMENT: SOME REFLECTIONS ON EXECUTIVE SEARCH AND THE PERSONNEL POLICIES OF JAPANESE SUBSIDIARIES IN GERMANY

H-J. Heise,
Eurosurvey

The executive search business in Germany has been growing steadily during the last 25 years and this reflects the growing importance of qualified personnel who exactly fit the standards and requirements of the company. It also demonstrates that the competition to hire the best qualified people has been steadily intensifying. Regarding the number, size, growth, image and importance of the Japanese companies in Germany, the number of assignments they place with professional executive search companies in Germany is much below the corresponding figures for American, British and German companies.

A study by one of the biggest US-based accounting and consulting firms says: not only do many Japanese managers in the United States have trouble relating to their American employees, they don't know how to recruit them either. The study found that many Japanese companies seeking to recruit American managers stress factors that are unimportant to Americans. Japanese managers, on the other hand, do not for example take as serious problems the Americans' fears of a foreign boss, Japanese management style and limited promotion prospects. But many qualified American managers list these as significant barriers to working for a Japanese company.

The same can be said about the situation in Germany for Japanese subsidiaries. It might thus be advisable for Japanese management to try to take into account these anxieties in their efforts to recruit top German talent, instead of hiring second class people who can live with these problems or who do not realise they are problems for their future careers and job satisfaction.

Concerning the still growing number of Japanese subsidiaries in Germany this has a very important consequence for those Japanese companies already working in Germany and those to come: due to the fact that there are already about 500 to 600 Japanese companies in Germany, more and more German managers therefore know, either from experience or from former colleagues and also from the press, about daily life at work, business practices and corporate culture in the Japanese subsidiaries as seen and experienced by the German management. And this will lead to a shortage of German talent for Japanese companies, because those who are qualified enough to have a challenging job offer from German and American companies will only in rare cases apply for a job in a Japanese subsidiary in Germany. This fact should cause Japanese management to formulate and practice an aggressive personnel marketing strategy in order to be able in the future to attract and to recruit first class local management.

Mr Peter Schutz, Chairman of the famous sports car manufacturer Porsche recently gave a speech at the German-American Chamber of Commerce in New York. From my point of view he formulated the basic elements of an aggressive personnel marketing strategy in saying, 'When we succeed in attracting and employing the best people in our market (recruitment policy!), when we give to them not only the facilities thy need to do their best, but succeed in motivating them (personnel policy!), we can adapt the company successfully to all future developments in a changing world'.

Most Japanese companies in Germany try to fill management vacancies via newspaper advertising. We believe newspaper advertising to be inappropriate and inefficient not only at boardroom and key executive levels, but also when in search of specialists in sales, marketing, technical fields and commerce. Newspaper advertising means communicating only with job hunters who represent only a small proportion of potential candidates. By doing so a company runs the real and substantial risk of spending time and money without making an appointment or appointing a person who, while reasonably competent, is not of the calibre of a select few, who could have been available if they had been searched out and approached via executive search. Therefore Japanese management in Germany has often recruited second or even third class people, because the first class was not available due to the channel used.

Japanese management in Germany often has only vague ideas concerning the professional experience and personnel traits of first class German management talent, because via newspaper advertising the chance to interview such top candidates is very limited. So it often happens that Japanese managers who work for the first time with an executive search company are surprised by the calibre of the candidates presented, because they have never met such candidates applying for a job in the company before. In addition,

Japanese management in Germany quite often has only vague ideas in respect of the qualifications of the management team of their competitors, because via newspaper advertising the chance to interview top talent from a competitor is very limied.

Japanese managers in Germany have great difficulties in interviewing candidates for a vacancy in their company. In order to assess a candidate carefully it is absolutely necessary to read between the lines of his curriculum vitae and to interpret the career moves of the candiates in a meaningful way. Japanese managers tend to overrate candidates coming from a competitor. Concerning the nonverbal behaviour of a candidate, most Japanese engaged in the selection process have no feeling for it.

The overwhelming majority of Japanese managers in Germany do not speak German. Therefore Japanese management often has little sensitivity concerning the working climate, rumours and gossip in the company. That means they barely have the chance to influence or to correct it efficiently. Therefore they also have great difficulties in influencing the informal structure of the company, because organisation charts do not tell the whole story of company interaction. A hive of informal groups penetrates the formal structure and affects it in many important ways. To run a company also means to run the informal structure but the greater the number of Japanese managers working in a German subsidiary the more class structured is the company and consequently the informal structure runs its own life. The Japanese managers tend to concentrate on their own ethnic group in the organisation and therefore often neglect the basic needs of the local management in respect of communication and motivation. This negative effect is quite often found when a company runs into difficulties and needs a strong, success-oriented and motivated local management instead of more Japanese 'supervisors'.

Japanese managers interviewing potential candidates for a management position in their German subsidiary in many cases only inform candidates very vaguely about the specific elements of Japanese management style and business culture as practised in Germany. So, when the new man has just started his job these surprising basics of Japanese management will lead to the first frustrations and discrepancies in expectation.

Japanese managers when interviewing candidates often present the company and the job very poorly. We have learned as executive search consultants that many German managers have joined a Japanese subsidiary not because of a convincing interviewing and screening procedure; instead they have signed the contract in spite of it. It is quite easy to imagine what this says about the candidate.

It is quite often neglected in Japanese subsidiaries in Germany that the new man needs the most motivation during his initial period in the company.

English-speaking Japanese managers in Germany only seldom have reliable contact with those employees who do not speak English. Therefore German managers have a chance to blame the Japanese management for all the negative developments in the company and even for their own mistakes and inadequacies. On the other hand, Japanese managers blame German managers when company targets can not be reached, but in many cases they have hired local managers, who objectively speaking have been the wrong calibre for this special kind of job.

The behaviour described in this paper often results in conflicts. The Japanese avoid conflict but they must learn that social conflict initiates change and development. Where conflict is suppressed or managed only in outward appearance social change and development of the company is hindered. Therefore German and Japanese personnel have to be trained in one another's business practices, managerial approaches and behavioural differences. This will significantly improve employee morale and sharply reduce cross-cultural misunderstandings and conflict.

Professional executive and long-term collaboration with an executive search consultant who is experienced in international and Japanese business in Germany can considerably reduce these difficulties.

INNOVATIONS IN COLLECTIVE BARGAINING THROUGH THE MULTINATIONALISATION OF JAPANESE AUTO COMPANIES. THE CASES OF NUMMI (USA) AND NISSAN (UK)

Knuth Dohse
Science Centre, Berlin

Multinational companies and national systems of industrial relations

There is a broad - potential as well as scientific - discussion about multinational corporations and their effect on national systems of industrial relations. The main issue is whether multinational corporations import elements of industrial relations into the host countries which are alien to the social and cultural patterns that have historically developed. The evidence on this question is inconclusive. Generally speaking one can distinguish two basic positions(1):

The first position argues - in line with widespread union thinking - that the very fact of subsidiary dependence on central headquarters introduces a new power structure into the labour relations arena. Making threats to withdraw and reallocate production is much more open to multinational companies compared to nationally focused firms. Through this there is also some potential for the transfer of management practices into the host countries which could and often do conflict with the national industrial relations system.

This basic thesis is more pronounced in Britain than e.g. in West Germany and focusses largely on US companies.

The second position argues, more in line with publicly pronounced management statements, that multinational companies have to adjust to the respective national industrial relations context. Headquarters are too removed from particular social and cultural aspects of the host countries to make sound judgements in fields like labour relations. This area is therefore better left to local management. Central management control runs the risk of making mistakes, which could result in inefficiency and disruption. Thus, multinational corporations do not basically change anything in the labour relations setting.

There are certainly also middle-ground theories. Two of them, it seems to me, are especially interesting, namely:

1. The life cycle thesis
2. The comparative control thesis.

The life cycle thesis (2) argues that multinational companies will initially be set up on a central control and dependency basis. Through the growth process of subsidiaries and the corresponding learning process, the dependency relationship is transformed into interdependency, giving more weight to local government and thus also to adjustment to national labour relations. The comparative control thesis (3) argues that multinational corporations, especially those producing similar products with similar technology in different countries, monitor plant performance on a comparative basis and will thus put central pressure on the less efficient operations to improve. While it is true that central management would run a high risk by intervening in nationally sensitive areas, central staff still have a powerful yardstick by which to monitor subsidiaries. Through central investment decisions they lend power to this monitoring exercise which is not readily available to nationally based firms. This performance pressure then has indirect effects on decentrally handled labour relations.

Present theories, for obvious reasons, largely concentrate on American multinationals. In this paper I would like to draw attention to the multinationalisation of Japanese auto companies and take up some of the issues raised. The life cycle thesis should, however, warn us that we might presently just be witnessing the pre-maturity phase which could be transformed over time. If we continue to observe these developments we would, however, also enlarge our general understanding of the relations between multinational corporations and national bargaining systems.

The drive to multinationalisation of Japanese auto companies

We have in the past ten years witnessed a dramatic increase in Japanese auto production. The major part of this growth was achieved through an enormous export offensive (Figure 1). The figures of the reshuffling of the world auto market are well known facts here.

What is important is that Japanese auto companies have in the past almost exclusively served the world market from their home territory. The most important single market in this respect was the North American continent, followed by Europe (?). The high export ratio of the Japanese auto industry opens up an extremely vulnerable spot: trade protection. The Japanese auto industry is in this respect even more vulnerable than the West German, which exports a higher ratio but mainly to the quasi-international EC market. Import protection would not just block the growth process in Japan, and thereby endanger a basic pre-requisite for the amazing stability of Japanese prodiction arrangements, but would also drastically curb the profitability of Japanese auto companies.

As is also well known, the Japanese export drive has stimulated quite an array of protectionist devices:

The import of Japanese cars into Great Britain is limited to around 11 per cent of the market.
Imports into France are limited to a 3 per cent market share.
Italy only allows 2,000 vehicles into its home market.

The major threat to the growth perspective of the Japanese auto companies, however, came, when the U.S. government arranged voluntary import restraint at 1.7 million vehicles. This figure was introduced in 1982 in the trough of the recession. Since, even after the increase to 1.85 million in 1984, it referred to an absolute number instead of a market percentage figure, Japanese companies were also unable to raise exports to the booming US car market of 1984-85. Thus overall Japanese exports stagnated from 1981 onwards and with them, due to a saturated home market, Japanese auto production altogether.

This situation has led to a drastic reconsideration of locational policies by Japanese auto firms. Almost every Japanese company is increasing its 'overseas' investment, setting up production plants outside Japan and thus becoming truly multinational companies. A particular emphasis is being put on the huge North American market. We presently witness a rush to North American locations, which is bound to lead to repercussions throughout the world auto industry. If present plans materialise, we will see one of the largest industrial relocation exercises ever occuring in the timespan of just a few years.

Honda has led the way by setting up a car production plant alongside its motorcycle assembly plant in Ohio in spring 1983. It is presently planning to double its capacity to around 300,000 in 1988. Nissan followed in 1984 by introducing car production into its Tennessee truck assembly plant. Capacity is planned to be increased to around 125,000 in 1988. The GM/Toyota joint venture started production in 1984 and will reach its 250,000 capacity in 1985. Toyota itself is presently looking for a site to set up an assembly plant in the US, which will be able to produce 200,000 cars from 1988 onwards. On top of this a Canadian plant for 50,000 cars is being planned.

Mazda has already chosen a site at Flat Rock, Michigan, which could build 250,000 cars from 1987 onwards.

Mitsubishi is heading for a joint project with Chrysler to build around 250,000 cars from 1987 onwards.

Isuzu and Suzuki are considering setting up assembly plants in Canada of unknown size. It these plans are realised, as now seems certain, the Japanese auto companies will have set up a North American subsidiary system of a total capacity of around 1.3 million vehicles within five years. This is roughly the size of the total British auto industry.

This rush to the U.S. will dramatically change the total international auto production and trade system. It is a situation of high risks and challenges for every actor involved:

1. For the Japanese auto companies one of the new issues will be, whether through US production they will take a larger bit off US companies or eat up part of their own exports. Although they continually tell their workforce that production in Japan will not be affected, quite a few American experts doubt this. GM's chief economist, for instance, is, from his point of view, optimistic: 'So unless there is a tremendous shift in demand towards small cars, a great deal of the output from Japanese factories in the US will substitute for imports. Otherwise the numbers just don't add up'(4). For the Japanese auto companies also the test comes up whether they can be as productive in other national and cultural contexts as in Japan.
2. The American auto companies have to envisage massive overcapacity on home territory. The highly respected broker firm Salomon Brothers calculates that in 1988 the US market share of American owned companies will drop from the present 70 per cent to just below 60 per cent. They calculate an overcapacity in the same year of around three million cars. (Table 1). This amounts to roughly three quarters of the total West German auto industry. This, as the consulting firm Paine and Webber point out, could easily lead to a 'bloodbath' in the next recession.(5)
3. The Japanese workforce is faced with the prospect that the tremendous growth period which stabilised the Japanese industrial relations system will almost certainly be over.
4. For the UAW (United Auto Workers) the rush of Japanese

auto companies into the US is partly a solution, partly a new problem. It is a solution in so far as jobs lost through imports can partly be picked up. It is a new problem, since the union-avoidance strategy pursued by Japanese companies so far, poses a severe threat to the overall viability of the union.

In my US related part I want to concentrate on the last point. Specifically I would like to put emphasis on the GM/Toyota joint venture NUMMI (New United Motor Manufacturing Incorporated), which has managed to involve the UAW in an innovative collective agreement. Massive Japanese investment in the US will, however, also have repercussions in Europe. If there is a continuing squeeze on exports from Japan to the US (through import restrictions, through production in North America, or through both) one can easily expect the Japanese companies to launch a stronger export drive towards Europe. Since this, however, could in turn lead to even stricter import controls, it is also very possible that the Japanese auto companies will have, with a due time lag, to follow the US route and place auto plants in European countries.

Here, as in the US, Nissan is the more multinationally minded company. This is certainly due to the tremendous pressure which is exerted on Nissan in the Japanese market by Toyota. In this respect there is a close parallel to Ford, which is also considerably smaller in the North American market but stronger in multinational ties compared to GM. After entering joint ventures with Alfa Romeo and taking the majority shareholding in Motor Iberica, Nissan is now setting up a new plant in Britain, which will start small scale production in summer 1986. Although it is not nearly as advanced as, for example, the Nissan project in the US, there are already tremendous expectations surrounding this experiment. It is expected that Nissan will be an impetus towards change in British management practice and the modernisation of the British industrial relations context.

I would therefore, secondly, like to draw attention to these expectations, to the factors behind them and to the first steps in developing a new bargaining and working system at Nissan UK.

The case of NUMMI

As was already mentioned in last year's paper(6), the companies that led the way into the US, Nissan in Tennessee and Honda in Ohio, went to great lengths to stay union-free. This strategy is based on the widely shared diagnosis that established union rules are a decisive factor in lower productive efficiency in the US compared to Japan. Seniority rules often make internal allocation of jobs and personnel a cumbersome and inefficient affair. Job demarcation and elaborate job classifications are a restrictive factor on the high utilisation of manpower. In this anti-union attitude itself, the Japanese companies so far are, neutrally speaking, an innovative factor in American auto production. But it might very well be that this is a short-sighted strategy.

The massive location plans of Japanese companies have already forced the UAW to put increased emphasis on organising Japanese owned plants. The first unionisation vote in Honda's Ohio plant is coming up in the near future. Inasmuch as these plants, because of supplier networks, are concentrated in specific areas, even in the South, the organisation drive will be facilitated. It is then very possible that unionisation against the company would result in less favourable contracts than if the companies had cooperated with the UAW from the start.

The experience of the GM Oklahoma plant is a case in point. GM set up this plant in 1978 in a Southern state with weak union influence and tried hard to stay union-free. It was felt that new productive work arrangements could only be developed without union interference. When the plant, after enormous pressure from the unionised plants of GM, was finally organised, it had, however, to agree to a contract, which in many respects was more cumbersome to handle than others. Original distrust was responsible for this. It is now widely felt in GM that the anti-union strategy was a basic mistake and that an innovative agreement in a green field plant could have been achieved with union involvement from the outset.

All that the lead companies Nissan and Honda have proved so far is that you can be very efficient on American territory. The proof of the pudding, however, that you can be efficient and respect the union at the same time, was left to NUMMI, the GM/Toyota joint venture. A great deal of attention is therefore focused on this plant. Brody expressed the general feelings very well in Fortune Magazine in July 1984(7):

> On the line ... is the prestige of Japan's No.1 automaker, embarked on its first major overseas manufacturing venture, and of the job-hungry United Auto Workers, which has never before organised a Japanese plant. In the longer run much more is at issue. As a cooperative endeavour between a symbol of Japanese efficiency and a powerful US union, New United Motor is the most important labour relations experiment in the US today. If Toyota can succeed in producing a car to Japanese quality standards at near Japanese costs

using unionised US workers, the venture could force profound changes on the rest of the US auto industry -and perhaps on other industries as well.

The joint venture was agreed on in February 1983 after 11 months of secret negotiations. The new joint company was planned with an investment of 300 million dollars. GM contributed its idle Fremont plant. This plant once employed 5,700 workers, and was completely renovated in April 1981 to accommodate the new front wheel drive A car, but had to be successively slimmed down until it finally closed in March 1982. Toyota was to introduce Japanese manufacturing techniques and to fill the major top management posts. The new plant was planned to produce 200,000 subcompact cars per year with 2,500 hourly employees, including personnel for a new built stamping plant.

As one can see from the 1983 analysis by Harbour and Associates (Table 2) this manpower goal amounted to a 50 per cent reduction in labour as compared to an average GM plant in the US. A considerable part of this saving could only be achieved if conventional work rules could be avoided. Through largely filling top positions with Japanese managers it was clearly demonstrated that the main test was going to be whether, in GM chairman Roger Smith's words, 'The Toyota manufacturing system, including just-in-time, could be made to work in the US'(8).

It was thus clear from the outset that the efficiencies aimed at could only be achieved if the UAW was prepared to enter a new arrangement. Therefore it was spelled out from the beginning that the final decision to go ahead would depend on 'the negotiation of a satisfactory labour agreement'(9).

In order to achieve this it was strongly pointed out that if one does not have a green field plant, one has at least a green field company with no previous contractual traditions. 'What we have here', Roger Smith pointed out during the signing ceremonies in February 1983, 'is a brand new company. We wanted to start it without any legal obligations (meaning the current GM-UAW contract). Nobody wants to handicap the operation with legal impediments. We will sit down and talk about the labour situtation with the UAW'(10).

However, because it was not a green field site, the UAW was at the same time in much greater trouble over making a compromise. It was confronted with the demands of previous Fremont employees for preferential hirings in line with the seniority-based recall rules of the local contract. Toyota chairman Toyoda's statement, that the entirely new company 'was also entirely free in its hiring policies', gave UAW leaders the chance to adopt a militant posture. UAW president Doug Frazer threatened that to operate Fremont without UAW members meant 'war'. And in his retirement speech at the 1983 UAW convention he stressed:

> You are talking about a plant that had 6,000 General Motors' workers; a plant that has been there for many years; that is going to produce a car that has a Chevy nameplate on. I think we have to say that not one single car will pull off the assembly line unless the former GM workers are on that line(11).

Statements like these certainly made clear that GM itself would be in trouble if the joint venture disregarded the UAW. They should, however, not blind us to the fact that the Union itself was prepared for a new deal. There are quite a number of reasons for that:

1. The UAW was a shocked as anybody in the US car industry by the slump in car production between 1978 and 1982. Auto production was reduced by 46 per cent whereas imports were increasing. The cost comparison exercise with Japan had convinced the UAW of the need for concessions, as witnessed by the agreements of 1982.
2. Outscouring strategies of US companies and the prospect of imports from Japan by American-owned companies had led to a strong motive to prove or reestablish the profitability of producing on American territory in a union environment.
3. Organising one company with Japanese affiliations was also regarded as a prerequisite for eventually organising the others.
4. There is finally a strong motive to find the positive aspects of the Japanese system, especially improved job protection.

This willingness to enter a new bargaining arrangement first became apparent when a letter of understanding between the UAW and the joint venture was signed in September 1983. Fremont would recognise the UAW. In turn the UAW would recognise that it was dealing with a new company and had to develop a new agreement. While the plant would mainly hire previous Fremont employees, the UAW accepted an intensive screening process (including assessment centres) and did not insist on previous seniority rights. To achieve this the UAW declared the Fremont local UAW organisation defunct and any rule books, union charts and agreements invalid, against heavy local opposition, including court action(12). On this basis the UAW and NUMMI entered an interim agreement. In April 1985, a few months after the start up of the operation, this resulted in a formal agreement, which for a running plant has many unprecedented features:

In order to put the changes into perspective, I would like to characterise briefly the traditional communication and employment systems in US auto plants. The traditional pattern is based on three factors:

1. An adversarial relationship with authoritarian management and confrontational union policies.
2. Hire and fire policies, but strictly according to seniority status.
3. Rigid internal manpower allocation bound by job classifications and demarcation rules.

All three factors are interrelated. Against authoritarian management, oriented towards management rights, the unions have over time put up a whole array of formalised hard to stay union-free. It was felt that neregulations binding management. Arbitrary hire and fire policies in the past were pushed back through formalised seniority provisions, which became more powerful over time. In order to safeguard employees against arbitrary transfer within the plants, the union has extended seniority rules to the internal labour market. The established division of labour was rigidified through job classifications and job demarcation, which protect employees against the arbitrary reallocation of tasks and at the same time, through safeguarding particular job categories especially in the area of skilled trades, also against layoffs.

The NUMMI contract, in contrast to this, develops a new triad:

1. Participation and cooperation.
2. Employment security.
3. Flexible manpower allocation.

Participation

The agreement(13) is based on the common understanding that the company's success and the progress of union members 'are to a large extent interdependent.' It therefore contains the common goal of 'building and maintaining the most innovative and harmonious labour-management relationship in America' (Section I.1.1).

Through 'working together as a team', 'full communication over the established policies and procedures', and through providing 'workers a voice in their own destiny in decisions that affect their lives before such decisions are made', there is a common commitment to 'build the highest quality automobile in the world at the lowest possible cost to the consumer' (Section I.1.3). Participation in company affairs is regulated in the following way:

1. There will be regular broad information on long-range plans and policies, quarterly production schedules, contemplated insourcing or outsourcing decisions and technological or major organisational change (Section I.1.4).
2. There will be no changes relating to personnel policies prior to a company union conference (Section I.1.4).
3. In order to develop continuous communication, there will be regular joint meetings at the company level and at the level of work sections. The agenda is open to both parties (Section IX).
4. In order to solve conflicts, especially in the field of health and safety as well as work standards, joint conflict resolution procedures are set up (Sections XXV, XXVIII). These conflict solution procedures substitute for the strike threat which, in other American automobile contracts, is left open in health and safety as well as work standard matters. Instead there is a definite no strike clause in the agreement viz:

   During the tem of this Agreement or any extension thereof, neither the Union nor its agents or representatives will cause, engage in or authorise its members to engage in any strike, sympathy strike, work stoppage, picketing, boycott, sick-out, slowdown or other concerted activity to interrupt work against the company.' (Section XXXVII.1.2).

According to the regional UAW director this arrangement carries potential risks and rewards for both sides:

> ...the parties agree to share all risk, responsibility and reward of partnership. We share the risk in that the union agrees to abandon part of its traditional re-active, adversial role in favour of a pro-active advocacy role, while the company surrenders some of its traditional management prerogatives in favour of conferring with the union on important issues(14).

Job security

The company pledges 'that it will not lay off employees unless compelled to do so by severe economic conditions that threaten the long-term viability of the company.' (Section III). While not formally guaranteeing life-long employment, this statement and the context in which it is embedded will ensure that NUMMI will risk the whole new productive arrangement and run into heavy conflict if it fires workers. Before any such action is taken the company will, according to the agreement, reduce management salaries, take back subcontracted work and solicit voluntary separations. This is certainly the first time a US auto company has stepped away from the easy lay-off principle.

Job flexibility

Participation and job protection can be regarded as the price to be paid to the union for accepting job flexibility. The most important innovation consists in the avoidance of the traditional elaborate job classification system. Instead there will be just one production classification and three skilled trade categories. It is agreed that the company will utilise a team concept of five to ten members each (Section XIV).

> 'All members of the team share responsibility for the work performed by the team and for participation for Quality/Productivity Improvement Programmes such as QC circles and KAIZEN' (Section XIV.1.1).

In order to gain the skills to complete every job in the group, team members are expected to rotate their jobs. A team leader will coordinate the process. The major advantage of the team concept for the company lies in its potential for saving manpower by adding previously separate tasks like quality inspection, materials handling and product repair to production jobs. The savings estimated by Harbour and Associates can be seen in Table 3. At the same time it is expected that teams will participate not only in quality improvement but also in reducing standard times.

> For some time prior to the execution of this Agreement the Company has been utilising a procedure for establishing and changing Standardised Work. Under this procedure, ... based on Toyota Production Methods, employees are encouraged and expected to participate with their Team Leaders and Group Leaders in designing and establishing Standardised Work' (Section XXVIII.1.1).

The original production control time standards are expected to be reduced through the teams' self-evaluation process. This exercise is called KAIZEN.

> Standardised Work is changed through a time data evaluation by the Team Leader and Group Leader. KAIZEN is performed to reduce required time for accomplishment to the target' (Appendix C, 2.8).

If a worker cannot perform his task he can sound an alarm and ultimately stop the line.

On the whole, we witness the attempt of a tremendous efficiency drive facilitated through union participation and through reducing the fear of lay-offs, which are largely regarded as responsible for workers not cooperating in efficiency improvements.

Under new arrangements the union now:

> Accepts the responsibility to promote the common objectives and to cooperate with the Company in administering, on a fair and equitable basis, standards of conduct; attendance plans and Problem Resolution; to promote constant improvement in quality and productivity; and to cooperate with the Company in dealing with governmental entities (Section II.1.5).

NUMMI is still at the experimental stage. Most people involved still seem to be quite enthusiastic about the new approach. But it still has to be seen to what extent American workers are willing to pay the price of giving up a fair amount of their control of the labour process. This contract has, of course, attracted a great deal of attention and is already serving as a model for others. The agreement which the UAW reached with the new GM daughter Saturn Corporation, followed the NUMMI line in many ways. It should, however, also be pointed out that the agreement falls in line with a general transformation of the American industrial relations system. The three basic elements of the new production arrangement have all been previously laid out.

A new drive towards participation is evident in the large scale Quality of Working Life and Employee Involvement programmes which GM and Ford started in 1982. The idea to trade improved job protection against increased internal labour flexibility was also launched in 1982, when GM and Ford agreed to test job security provisions in three plants each. With the established pattern of industrial relations, however, these concepts proved very difficult to get off the ground. None of the model plants have come up with a new compromise.

NUMMI therefore is not so much innovative in the sense that it has created totally new ideas. It is innovative in the sense that it is the first to integrate new concepts in a working plant and has thus opened them up for learning and experience. Thus NUMMI is certainly not the prime mover in changing industrial relations in the United States. It might, however, through setting an example, speed up the process.

The case of Nissan UK

If the Nissan plant in the UK stays as small as is presently planned for its pilot phase, it would hardly be worth talking about. This pilot phase, beginning with the production start up in mid 1986, involves the assembly of 24,000 Nissan cars per year. As such, it rather resembles a KD plant (knocked down vehicle assembly), which is typically placed in underdeveloped countries. It is, as Automotive News put it in February 1984, 'the sort of plant that Nissan has built in South East Asia and Africa'(15).

But to stay at this level of investment would not make much sense to the company itself. The main motive in building a plant in Europe is very similar to that for setting up plants in the US: namely to become an insider company in the EC and thereby to enlarge its market share, limited so far by the import restrictions of some of the important member countries. The output of the pilot plant, however, is classified as Japanese and will not serve this purpose: so the setting up of the pilot plant is rather meant to provide a test ground under uncertain circumstances. It serves the purpose of making sure that conditions are satisfactory to go ahead in building a fully fledged production complex. When Nissan first announced the idea of setting up production facilities in Britain in January 1981, it was talking about a 200,000 car production complex including a stamping plant and machining facilities(16). These plans not only ran into heavy opposition from British producers and into long drawn out debates over local content rules and government subsidies, they also encountered escalating conflicts between the Nissan union chief Shioji and the Nissan top manager Ishihara. When the decision was finally made three years later in February 1984, it resulted in a much more cautious, longer term and try-out style commitment. Altogether it represents a 3-stage concept:

Stage I is the pilot project, starting in summer 1986. Production will move up to 24,000 cars per year, mainly assembly of Japanese kits. 400 to 500 direct jobs will be created through an initial investment of £50 million. The pilot project will, according to Automotive News, 'ascertain the feasibility of future development of the project to gain experience in management and labour practices, sourcing of local components and other operating conditions in the UK'(17). In summer 1987 a decision based on this experience will be made whether to go ahead with Stage II.

Stage II will then lead up to 1990 and an increase in production up to 100,000 cars per year. It will start with 60 per cent EC content and move up to 80 per cent. The cars will then count as British and will therefore be free of the import restrictions of other EC countries. It is expected that Nissan UK will provide 2,700 direct jobs during this phase(18).

Why Britain was chosen as the EC country to invest is open to speculation but there may be three main types of reason:

1. Britain is by now an established member of the EC. If local content requirements are fulfilled this would provide immediate access to the EC market. Investing in Spain, the other obvious choice for a company like Nissan, might have resulted in retaliatory action by potential export countries because it still protects its national car market against EC competitors.

2. The UK government was extremely keen to have a Japanese auto company, widely respected for their efficiency, come to Britain. In a phase, when Britain was losing an important part of its industrial base, a full scale Nissan plant would, as the Financial Times put it, 'be by far the largest manufacturing investment to come Britain's way in the past few years'(19). The Government could easily make such an investment a sign that it was finally on the right track. In addition, it hoped that a Japanese producer in Britain, through settting a competitive example, would help the government's attempts to make British industry more competitive as well as to change the industrial relations system. Norman Tebbit, then Secretary of State for Trade and Industry, has from the outset argued, as the Financial Times reported, 'that Nissan would give the UK motor industry a

shot in the arm by introducing Japanese Management techniques(20). And after the deal the Sunday Times reported that 'privately ministers hope that it will act as a catalyst in the reform of labour relations practices elsewhere in the motor industry'(21). This is very much in line with what the Nissan chairman, Kawamata, had to say about his contact with the British government. In the January 1984 issue of the Oriental Economist he was quoted as follows:

When I went to Europe in 1983, the British Secretary of Trade and Industry expressed a wish to see me. I asked him bluntly, 'You are very eagerly inviting Nissan to advance into Britain. This is very strange to me. What is your reason? He answered in the following way: 'Nissan has acquired very new production. It has good labour-management relations. Everything is an object of envy for us. We want you to set up your operation in Britain to demonstrate not only to our automakers but also to other industries these aspects of Japanese management'. When I heard this I thought in my mind: 'Of all the things, they just want us to be a tutor at their home. If we are to be that ... they should pay us return air fare, our expenses during our stay in Britain and a very big salary.' They are expecting too much in asking us to tutor them at our own expense'(22).

In fact Nissan did not just get the return air fare. It is estimated that Nissan has obtained government subsidies of around £112 million towards the £350 million costs of the Stages I and II investment.

3. Because of high unemployment there is quite a supply of well trained skilled engineering labour available in Britain. Additionally, this labour is relatively cheap. Compared to West Germany for instance, wages are roughly 30 per cent lower in Britain. If Nissan succeeded in setting up an efficiently manned operation in Britain, it would have a competitive advantage over many Continental locations.

The success of the new company, however, crucially depends on this last conditional statement. It is true that other Japanese manufacturers have been quite successful in Britain. But the complete investment package of Nissan would have quite another dimension:

> If the whole scheme goes ahead, the investment will be substantially larger than the total value of Japan's existing assets in the UK...

This size implies a particular risk. As Daniel Jones has shown for the seventies, there is a diseconomy of scale observable in Britain because of the particular labour relations situation. Thus, the Financial Times was certainly right, when it stated in 1982:

> A new, large scale car plant in a country well known for difficult labour relations represents a considerable risk for a company whose experience of manufacturing outside Japan is limited. Japanese companies which are alreay established in the UK have done well, but the Nissan project is of a different order of magnitude(24).

Because of this, labour relations issues played a crucial, but not always forefront, role in the debate on Nissan's investment plans in Britain. Already in January 1982 Okama, then Executive Vice President for overseas operations, stated:

> The only problem is how we will be able to manage the workforce well, avoiding disputes. If we can succeed, we shall have an edge over the established car manufacturers(25).

When the investment plans were shelved in mid 1982, a Nissan representative stated:

> We are getting the impression that maybe there is a change taking place among workers. Maybe they are beginning to take the offensive again after being on the defensive for the past two years - and are getting more inflexible(26).

The issues are certainly some of the underlying reasons for Nissan to start small and proceed with the stage concept. In any case, just as the implementation of the pilot project was subject to a 'satisfactory' union agreement, so are decisions to enter the next stage dependent on satisfactory efficiency levels of labour relations. Thus Kaichi Kanao, then Executive Vice President in charge of UK operations (presently Vice Chairman), told The Guardian:

> We certainly hope we will be able to accumulate the experience to go on to the next stage, but relations with the trade

union will be a big factor in determining whether to go ahead(27).

To obtain the desired efficiencies, Nissan was determined to avoid the trouble spots that other auto manufacturers find in Britain:

1. Job demarcation makes it more difficult for British producers to follow the efficiency trend by integrating direct and indirect functions, thus considerably saving manpower, compared to German or Japanese producers. Rules of 'excess mobility' restrict manpower allocation. Some of these features are similar to the situation in the US. The multi-union structure in Britain has, on top of this, made the lines of demarcation within skilled trades and between skilled trades and production workers particularly rigid.
2. 'Scientific' time standards are not nearly as accepted in Britain as in the US or in West Germany. In the Seventies, and partly still today, the workload is a matter of informal bargaining at the shop floor.
3. Contrary to the US, but in line with West Germany, British companies would regularly risk trouble if they resorted to enforcing redundancies. Ford and Vauxhall have therefore relied on voluntary separations to cut their workforce.
4. Because of very little central union control, work sections can withhold their labour, and thus apply pressure to achieve their particular interests.

All of these factors, management claims, have led to substantial overmanning in Britain. But it is also true that management, in times of economic prosperity, was ready for an easy compromise. Labour in Britain was comparatively cheap and car prices were substantially higher than on the Continent. Thus, even overmanning can pay and did pay. Under the new competitive pressure of the late Seventies and the Eighties, this arrangement has, however, collapsed.

It is interesting to note that Nissan UK, contrary to Nissan US, did not try to stay union-free. Apparently management saw no chance to avoid the unions altogether in the British context. And interesting, too, is the fact, that, contrary to the experience of the established local car manufacturers, the multi-union situation in Britain turned out to be an advantage for Nissan. After insisting, for obvious reasons, on a green field site, Nissan placed the plant in a high unemployment area in the Northeast of Britain, which is apparently known for its 'favourable' labour relations climate:

'Labour relations in the town are generally good and in the Northeast as a whole, unions have begun to negotiate so called 'single factory' agreements - one union for each factory - to break down some of the traditional craft disciplines. This industrial relations record, more than anything, impressed Nissan'(28). Under the circumstances of high unemployment, the job-hungry northern TUC indicated to Nissan that, if investment were placed in the area, the company would be free to chose the individual union it wanted(29). Instead of inter-union disputes affecting company performance, Nissan was in a position to use the choice to its own advantage by picking the winner. It is obvious that a company in this situation would choose the union which would agree to the most favourable deal. Nissan had drafted a proposed agreement and presented it to the trade unions wishing to organise their new assembly plant. When the Amalgamated Union of Engineering Workers (AUEW) accepted it, it won the race. This single union deal already represents a major innovation in the British auto industry(30). The AUEW will have 'representation rights for all personnel up to and including senior engineers and equivalent levels employed by the Company' (Section 2a). This, of course, lays the basis for the integration of tasks which cut across conventional lines of representation and which other companies therefore find so hard to achieve. In order to safeguard the single-union situation, the company will encourage their workers to join this union.

A central element, as in the NUMMI contract, is job flexibility. This has many aspects and the company will start with a dual classification system for blue collar workers. The term 'manufacturers' will replace all production and most semi-skilled indirect classifications. Skilled workers will be called 'technicians', a term which will replace the conventional classifications of plumbers, machine tool repairmen, electricians etc. In order to gain new efficiencies, workers will be required to work in teams and to be responsible for quality control, materials handling, cleaning the workplace and minor maintenance in addition to line work. Technicians are required, with appropriate training, to perform tasks outside their conventional trade functions.

In addition, 'to ensure the fullest use of facilities and manpower there will be a complete flexibility and mobility of employees' (Section 11a). 'Manning levels will be determined by the company'(Section 11d). In contrast to NUMMI, where the wage system is rather traditionally structured, the wage structure of Nissan UK will be more flexible. The contract, as it stands, has not fully determined the wage system. It just states:

> A salary range will be established to apply to each occupational classification and progression through this range be related to the individual's performance (Section 10).

This, however, lays the basis for a wage system open to merit criteria and performance evaluation by management. This concept is probably the single most important factor that would have touched a raw nerve with other unions. As in NUMMI, there is considerable emphasis on 'promoting effective communication and harmonious relations between the company, its employees and the union' (Section 3a). For this purpose a joint Company Council will be established. It will have a threefold purpose (Sections 3; 5):

1. It acts as a consultative forum on company policies.
2. It is the final internal stage of dispute procedure before the matter is referred to ACAS for binding arbitration.
3. In separate sessions it will draw in the regional trade union officer and then act as the negotiating board.

In order to reinforce this arrangement the union accepts that there 'will be no industrial action of any kind while an issue is in procedure or the subject of conciliation or arbitration'(Section 6e). Since binding arbitration is the final stage of all disputes this clause amounts to a no-strike promise for the duration of the contract.

What is conspicuously absent from the agreement is an employment protection commitment, which is a central element of the NUMMI deal. Instead, the agreement only contains rather liberal regulations for the periods of notice for termination of employees. They range from one week during the probationary period to 12 weeks after 12 years of employment (Section 24).

Altogether the company very much got what it wanted. There is no new two-party arrangement in sight which also carries the fingerprint of the union. While this seems to be a sign of the company's strength in the founding period of the plant, it might very well turn out to be Nissan's weak spot. It is certainly possible that the AUEW took the chance to get into the plant and let management find out what happens afterwards. This has occurred at other companies for many years, where somewhat similar flexibility rhetoric was included in national agreements, only to leave the company to realise that it would not work in practice. This could, of course, also happen to Nissan. It is particularly questionable whether the AUEW, given its internal structure, could really deliver a no-strike clause. But even if we keep this in mind,

Nissan will have a favourable starting point for gaining comparatively high efficiency levels through its single union deal; and, of course, Nissan has some powerful aces up its sleeve through the upcoming investment decisions.

When we take up the question of to what exent the Nissan agreement is innovative, the single-union situation certainly stands out as a very important factor. In every other aspect Nissan has tied itself into an efficiency drive of all the British companies. The difference is not one of ideas. The difference is that, given local traditions and the established industrial relations structure, the other companies will find it extremely difficult to put them into practice. Through being a green-field company on a green-field site, Nissan certainly has a headstart in this efficiency campaign and, as such, we reencounter the same process which we have observed at NUMMI. If Nissan is successful, it might speed up the train which was already on the track before, because of the increased competitive pressure of the car industry in general.

Some final remarks

1. Both cases represent the initial stages of a longer term development process. It will take some years of observation to find out to what extent the new plants will need to adjust to local circumstances or rather to continue to serve as a yardstick for innovation.
2. In both cases there were no radical new ideas introduced into a foreign setting. Rather, the industrial relations system of the host country was already in motion in the same direction. Neither case turned the table around, but they could very well serve to speed up the process of change through increasing the competitive pressure.
3. Both cases are under the close monitoring of the mother companies, although under different circumstances. NUMMI, the full-fledged production complex, will have to live with two kinds of comparison: the comparison with Toyota home plants and the comparison with GM home plants. Here industrial engineering data from Toyota have directly entered American territory and also the bargaining arena. They will certainly also be utilised by GM if they are successfully applied. Nissan, due to differences in scale, cannot easily be measured against Japanese home plants; but in this case the central headquarters can possibly exert an even stronger pressure on performance levels through the upcoming investment decisions.

Notes

(1) See discussion in:
R.S. Flanagan and H.R. Weber (eds.), Bargaining without Boundaries. The Multinational Corporation and International Labour Relations, University of Chicago, London, 1974.
D. Kujawa, The Labour Relations of United States Multinationals Abroad: Comparative and Prospective Views, Research Series No.60, International Institute for Labour Studies, Geneva, 1980.
L. Otterbeck (ed.), The Management of Headquarters - Subsidiary Relationships in Multinational Corporations, Gower, Aldershot, 1981.
(2) For example, C. Prahalad and Y. Doz, 'Strategic Control - the Dilemma in Headquarters - Subsidiary Relationships', Otterbeck, op.cit., p.187, ff.
(3) For example, K. Dohse, U. Jürgens, T. Malsch, 'Fertigungsnahe Selbstregulierung oder zentrale Kontrolle - Konzernstrategien im Restrukturierungsprozess der Automobilindustrie'. In: Naschold, F. (Hg.), Arbeit und Politik, Campus Verlag, Frankfurt/New York 1985, pp.49-90.
(4) Financial Times, London, 5 September 1985.
(5) Ibid.
(6) U. Jürgens, K. Dohse, T. Malsch, Japan als Orientierungspunkt für den Wandel der industriellen Beziehungen in der US-amerikanischen und der europäischen Automobilindustrie, International Institute for Comparative Social Research, pre 84-224, Berlin, 1984.
(7) Fortune Magazine, 9 July 1984, p.48.
(8) Automotive News, 23 April 1984.
(9) Automotive News, 21 February 1983.
(10) Automotive News, 28 February 1983.
(11) Automotive Industries, July 1983, p.23.
(12) Automotive News, 12 September 1983.
(13) Agreement between New United Motor Manufacturing Inc. and the UAW, 1 July 1985.
(14) UAW, UAW-NUMMI. Special Report to the Membership, June 1985, p.2.
(15) Automotive News, 20 February 1984.
(16) Automotive News, 18 January 1982.
(17) Automotive News, 20 February 1984, p.6.
(18) My original analysis pointed to a three stage concept. The third stage would cover the 1990s and, depending on market conditions and other factors, production would advance above

the 200,000 figure. According to a personal communication of Mr Goto, General Manager of Nissan's London Office, however, there 'is no such stage'.

(19) Financial Times, London, 24 October 1983.

(20) Financial Times, London, 5 July 1982.

(21) Sunday Times, London, 28 April 1985.

(22) Financial Times, London, 2 February 1984. Also: B. Ridgers, The Nissan Factor, London, (mimeo), 1981, p.16.

(23) Financial Times, loc.cit.

(24) Financial Times, 21 July 1982.

(25) Automotive News, 15 January 1982, p.46.

(26) Financial Times, 1 September 1982.

(27) The Guardian, London, 31 March 1984.

(28) Ibid.

(29) Financial Times, London, 15 April 1985.

(30) Agreement and Conditions of Employment. Nissan Motor Mfg (UK) Ltd., and AUEW.

Table 1 Projections of US auto production and auto market

Units in thousands

	1985+	1986+	1988+	1990+
Capacities				
General Motors	5,000	5,000	5,150	5,400
Ford	1,800	1,800	1,800	1,800
Chrysler	1,350	1,350	1,350	1,350
AMC	135	135	135	135
Volkswagen	115	115	115	115
Honda	150	150	300	300
Nissan	70	70	125	125
NUMMI	80	250	250	250
Mazda			240	240
Mitsubishi			180	180
Toyota			200	200
Total capacity	8,700	8,870	9,845	10,095
US Manufacturers	95.2%	93.4%	85.7%	86.1%
Foreign Manufacturers	4.8	6.6	14.3	13.9
US Auto Sales‡	10.70	10.75	9.75	10.80
Imports‡	2.71	3.11	3.00	3.40
Domestic Sales‡	7.99	7.64	6.75	7.40
Excess Capacity	710	1,230	3,095	2,695
Operating Rate	92.0%	86.0%	69.0%	73.0%
Market share				
Imports	25.3%	28.9%	30.8%	31.5%
Foreign Production	29.7	34.6	40.7	41.6
US Production	70.3	65.4	59.3	58.4

‡In millions + Estimate

Source: Salomon Brothers; quoted in the Financial Times, 5 September 1985.

Table 2 NUMMI in comparison

Assembly plant compared

	Fremont, CA	Typical Japanese Plant	Typical New GM Plant
Daily production	800 cars	1000 cars	1200 cars
Size	2.9m ft^2	1.5m ft^2	3.0m ft^2
	269,700 m^2	139,500 m^2	279,000 m^2
Direct labour	1050	1112	2600
Indirect labour			
hourly	725	625	2125
salary	325	175	525
Total employment	2100	1912*	5250*
including stamping	2500	n/a	n/a
Total hours	16,800	15,300	42,000*
including stamping	20,000	n/a	n/a
Manhours labour/car	21	15.3*	35.0*
including stamping	25	n/a	n/a

* does not include stamping

Source: Harbour and Associates, quoted in Automotive Industries, May 1983, p. 16

Table 3 Manpower savings at Fremont

Title	Amount reduced
Quality inspectors	250
Relief men	
mass relief	280
lower absentees	220
Materials handlers	250
Repairmen	250
Union reps	40

Source: Harbour & Associates, quoted in Automotive Industries, May 1983, p. 16

These are six of the major categories where Toyota will be able to eliminate jobs. Further reductions will come from flexible work rules which will allow one worker to perform several jobs.

Figure 1 Japanese auto industry 1971-83

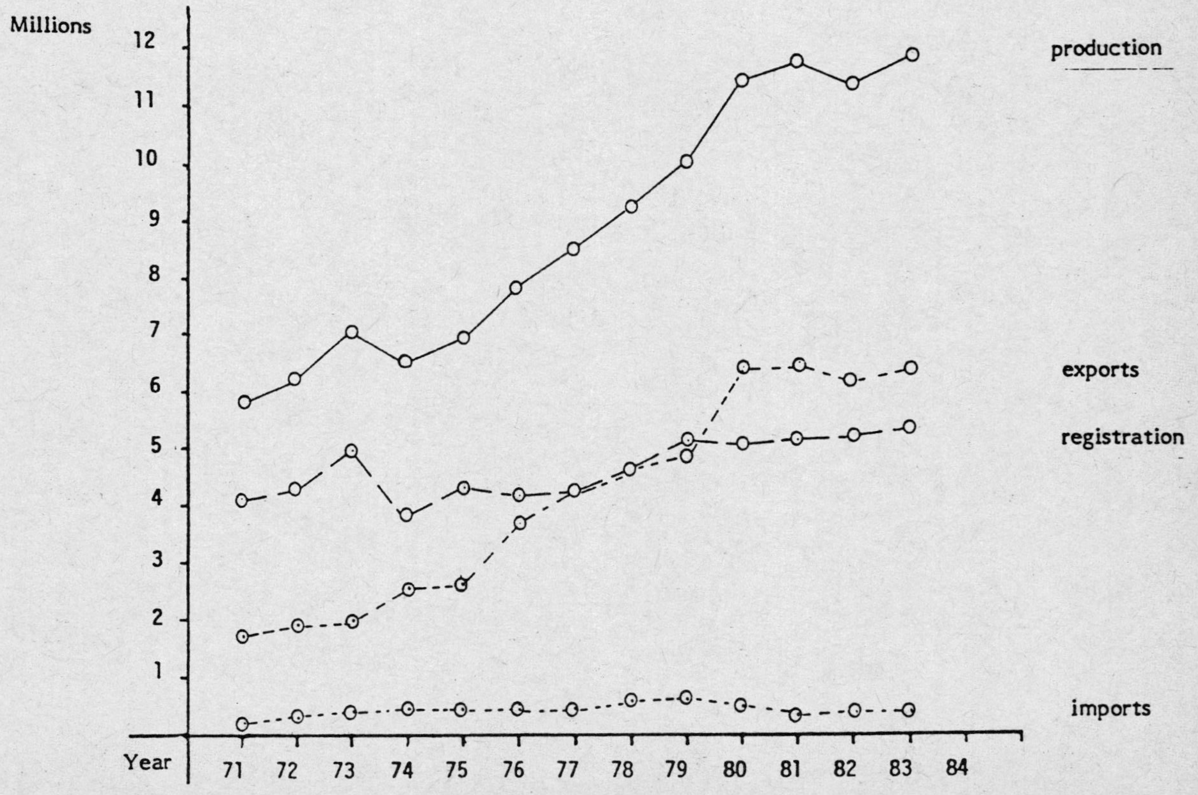

JAPANESE MARKET ENTRY STRATEGY. THE CASE OF YAMANOUCHI PHARMACEUTICALS IN WESTERN EUROPE

Y. Abe
Yamanouchi Pharmaceutical Co. Ltd.

Introduction

After the Second World War certain Japanese industries such as automobiles, cameras, consumer electronics and steel have rapidly strengthened their international base and some leading companies in these fields have already achieved their internationalisation and joined the so-called multinational enterprises (MNEs).

On the other hand, the Japanese pharmaceutical industry has lagged behind in internationalisation. The main reasons are:

1. The Japanese pharmaceutical technology was immature and R & D weak. Therefore, growth was based mainly on new products licensed from Western multinational pharmaceutical companies (MPCs).
2. Japanese companies had a growing domestic market, supported by the health and welfare system. They had no need to develop overseas markets.

However, the recent growing strength of Japanese pharmaceutical companies is one of the notable features of the world pharmaceutical industry. The Financial Times of December 29, 1983 stated that, 'For American and European drug companies the pressures are aggravated by stiffening competition from the Japanese who have targeted the sector as a crucial one for international growth. Traditionally strong in antibiotics, the Japanese are now moving into many other therapeutic areas'.

In addition to that, the market environment of the Japanese pharmaceutical industry is becoming more and more severe with the progress of government policies to improve the health insurance system and to curtail all medical expenditure. As a consequence, the industry experienced for the first time almost zero growth in drug production in 1983.

Under these circumstances, most of the major Japanese pharmaceutical companies are seeking the best way of expanding their business abroad; whether this is to proceed in the early stages with a licensing arrangement, to move into a joint venture or to adopt direct marketing.

The world pharmaceutical industry

The world pharmaceutical market in 1982 was estimated at US $80 billion. The largest market is the USA (approx. 25 per cent) followed by Japan (17 per cent), West Germany (8 per cent), France (7 per cent), Italy (4 per cent), the UK (4 per cent) and Spain (3 per cent). These markets have been dominated by a handful of US, Swiss and German MPCs.

Compared to these giants, the Japanese companies are still in the second division. Only one company, Takeda, can claim a place among the top 20.

The largest pharmaceutical company in the world is Hoechst (West Germany), whose pharmaceutical sales reached about $2,700 million in 1982, while Takeda's were US $1,300 million and Yamanouchi's US $390 million.

It can be said that the world pharmaceutical industry has enjoyed stable growth and high profitability. The Financial Times of June 2, 1982 pointed out that, 'The pharmaceutical industry has passed through the recession almost unscathed, such is the nature of its business. People continue to fall ill and to need drugs - no matter how harsh the economic climate - and the industry has therefore been able to maintain and often to improve its profitability'.

This logic is sound and the statement in fact describes what has happened to the industry. However this is not to suggest that the industry has no problems. The main factors impinging upon the pharmaceutical industry can be summarised as follows:

1. As a result of the rising cost of health care, governments are enforcing strict price controls on drugs in major markets.
2. New products are taking longer to emerge from the R & D stage and R & D costs are becoming much higher.
3. The regulations governing the safety standards of new drugs are being made stricter.

Despite these problems, there seems to be a general agreement among the people involved in the industry that the next three decades are likely to bring a second pharmaceutical revolution with control of cancer, diabetes etc. The pharmaceutical industry in the major countries will therefore continue to flourish during this future developmental phase, even though future advances will be enormously expensive.

The internationalisation of the Japanese pharmaceutical companies

Along with the rapid growth of MNEs a large number of empirical investigations and theoretical studies have been conducted with regard to the internationalisation of firms. These studies show that the process of internationalisation has the following sequence: exporting - licensing - establishing overseas sales subsidiaries - and establishing production facilities in foreign markets. The important characteristic of the process has been found to be a gradual one, and not the result of strategy but the consequence of incremental adjustments to the changing conditions of the firm and its environment.

Most of the Japanese pharmaceutical companies have been no exception to the theory. They have been achieving their internationalisation gradually and are still at the stage of licensing. In the US and Western Europe only a few joint ventures are currently operating.

In the US it seems that joint ventures have been the most common mode of entry. This can be attributed to the fact that the US market is too large for even the largest Japanese company, requiring more than 500 detailmen to cover the market.

On the other hand, Japanese companies have been adopting various entry methods to penetrate European markets, as they consist of many countries with different customs, languages, regulations and so on.

In the 1970s, major Japanese companies established their representative offices in Europe while they were expanding their business activities through licensing. Since then they have been shifting to direct investment in Europe.

Takeda, the largest Japanese pharmaceutical company, established joint ventures with Roussel Uclaf in France and with Grünenthal in West Germany. Otsuka and Eisai also established joint ventures in West Germany in 1984. More recently Tanabe has announced that it will establish a joint venture with Glaxo in the UK. In 1983 Fujisawa acquired a minority shareholding in Klinge Pharma in West Germany. Furthermore, Shionogi has established a wholly-owned subsidiary and Otsuka has set up its own R & D centre in West Germany.

It is evident that the preference of Japanese companies for West Germany is due to its market size; the largest market in Europe.

The history of Yamanouchi's internationalisation

Yamanouchi Pharmaceuticals was founded in 1923 in Osaka and started its internationalisation by exporting to the Far East in the 1950s.

In the Far East, the company has established its operations through exporting, licensing and a joint venture. Taiwan Yamanouchi, which was set up in 1963, is the sole joint venture that the company has in overseas markets.

In the US, the company has established licensing relationships with MPCs such as Merck and Co. and Syntex. In addition, in 1983 the company's future business base for the US and Canada was established by its long-term agreement with Eli Lilly. Yamanouchi's new products will be licensed to Eli Lilly and both parties have agreed to form a joint venture in the future.

In Western Europe, Yamanouchi has expanded its business activities mainly through licensing. Jasamycine (antibiotic) was first licensed to Pharmuka (France) in the mid-1970s, and has been launched in several European countries. Other new products including perdipine (calcium antagonist), Yamatetan (cephamycine antibiotic) and Atock (bronchodilator) have been licensed to Western MPCs such as Sandoz (Swiss), Ciba-Geigy (Swiss) and ICI (UK). More of these licensed products will be commercialised in 1985 and 1986.

The company established representative offices in New York in 1979 and in London in 1980.

Under these circumstances Yamanouchi has set its eye on Western Europe. The final target of the company is to develop, manufacture and sell its products independently in Western Europe.

Yamanouchi's entry strategy in Western Europe

When a firm has made up its mind to go abroad, it must consider different marketing strategies relating to international activities. The multinational marketing decision which Yamanouchi should add to the basic marketing functions for entering European markets can be shown as follows:

1. Choice of product

   The product which is used as a vehicle to enter foreign markets must be a self-developed new product now under development and one that has a large potential market. Fortunately, the R & D pipeline of the company is filling up with even more new self-developed drugs.

2. Choice of country
   Four major European countries - West Germany, France, UK and Italy should be selected as primary target markets by the single-variable screen method based on their market size. A further analysis of these markets is necessary to decide which country Yamanouchi should base its entry into Europe on. A country's characteristics, such as product size, political stability, regulations on drugs etc., and Yamanouchi's ability to compete must be considered when screening the country.

3. Mode of entry
   As noted elsewhere, Yamanouchi has expanded its business activities overseas through exporting and licensing.

According to the traditional internationalisation theory, Yamanouchi's next steps into Western Europe should be the establishment of a sales subsidiary, followed by the establishment of manufacturing facilities.

Several strategy options much be examined at this stage i.e. choice of ownership, the method of entry of the subsidiary into the parent organisation - setting up or acquisition, and business activities - sales subsidiary and/or manufacturing facility.

It goes without saying that these strategic choices must be examined by taking into account the factors peculiar to the firm and its industry.

Conclusion

Yamanouchi started its internationalisation by exporting gradually and steadily increasing its commitments to foreign markets. The literature indicates that this is mainly due to management's uncertainty caused by lack of knowledge and experience in foreign markets. It is apparent however that firms have been influenced by recent economic and other external environmental changes in international business, which have made the global economy more competitive. Furthermore, political and social intervention in the world economy have put international business in a more complex situation.

It seems unlikely that firms faced by a severely competitive environment can become prosperous in the world economy by gradual internationalisation. Rapid and strategic adjustment to the changing environment must be an essential condition for firms to survive.

Considering this point, and the managerial resources and the final target of Yamanouchi, the writer of the paper recommends the following entry strategy for the company:

1. The company should base its entry into Europe on the UK. The rating scale country screening method indicates that West Germany is the most attractive market for Yamanouchi, followed by the UK, France and Italy. However, the main factors in relation to Yamanouchi's ability to compete which influence the final decision are the language and the presence of the London office.
2. The company should set up a wholly-owned sales subsidiary in the UK. Considering the competitive situation in the pharmaceutical industry and the objectives of the company, it should select this policy and not be diverted by the advantages of a joint venture. Target countries for establishing a factory and/or an R & D facility should be screened based on other factors such as infrastructure, labour costs, availability of pure water and so forth.

THE THEORETICAL PROBLEMS OF THE TRANSFERABILITY OF MANAGEMENT STYLE

Yoshiaki Takahashi
Chuo University

Three factors that determine management style

Keichiro Nakagawa, former Professor of Business History at Tokyo University, has pointed out the three fundamental factors which determine the management style of a country, from the aspect of Enterprise History, namely: Cultural structure, economic process and the internal and external organisation of the enterprise(1). The cultural structure means the behavioural style, the life goal or value system of the individual person in a particular era and country. 'Homo Economicus', on which traditional economics has been based, is a model of the individual in one particular era and country which can not be adopted for the explantion of individual human behaviour in any era and in any country.

Arthur H. Cole, Joseph A. Schumpeter and Thomas C. Cochran of the 'Centre for Enterprise History Study', which was organised between 1949 and 1959, asserted that the analysis of capital and technology alone was not enough to make clear the concrete content of the economic development of a country, but that it was necessary to analyse the adaptability of its human behaviour style to economic development. It seems to be the case that these scholars were not satisfied with the assumptions of 'Homo Economicus'. The behaviour style or value system of the individual person in a particular era and country may be conditioned not only by the economic process and the internal organisation of enterprise, as Nakagawa mentioned, but also by the dominant religion, law and educational system of which the cultural structure of the country is composed. However, the speed of change of the behaviour, style or value system of the individual person must be more gradual than the other two factors.

The second factor, the 'economic process', means economic factors which condition the decision-making of the entrepreneur or manager. In order to be clear about the economic process concretely, in the context of the decision-making of an entrepreneur or manager of a particular country, it is not enough to analyse its progress only from the aspect of economic process, as the 'Industrial Revolution' or 'Industrialisation' of a country, was very different between the early developed countries of Europe and USA and the late developed countries, such as Japan etc., Alexander Gerschenkron's model explains these different phenomena fairly well.

Gerschenkron's model consists of the following four propositions:

(1) The later the industrialisation of a country is, the faster the speed of its industrialisation. This is because the late developer can introduce the newest production techniques from the starting point of its industrialisation which were developed by early developers over a long time; and also because the late developer can occasionally borrow capital from early developers where accumulation has been promoted.

(2) The industrialisation of the late developer must be promoted on a large scale from the strarting point. If the late developer cannot introduce the newest techniques at the same level and on the same scale as the early developer, the late developer cannot compete with the early developer on equal terms in the product market because of higher prices than those of the early developer.

(3) The industrialisation of the late developer must be guided by a certain strong institution at the national level. The existence of such an enterprise or national bank, which was seen in the phase of Japanese industrialisation in the Meiji Era, was an example of such a fact.

(4) 'Laissez-faireism', 'individualism' and 'rationalism', which were the ideas of the early developer, can not be applied to the late developer. Instead of these ideas the latter needs 'nationalism' or a 'semi-religious' idea(2).

Even if Gerschenkron's propositions may be adaptable to some extent in order to explain the process of Japan's industrialisation, it is doubtful whether this model can aptly explain the process of industrialisation in other late or hardly developed countries. Anyway, we cannot deny that the economic process is a factor that conditions the decision-making of the entrepreneur or manager.

The third factor, the internal and external organisation of the enterprise, is a relatively independent factor in determining management style. Because the development of a better enterprise cannot be attained unless the organisational behaviour fits into the cultural structure and the economic process, in spite of both being well conditioned, the organisation has the character of an organism and a historical substance in the sense of biological growth. The organism absorbs matter from the external world and expels waste matter. Likewise, the organisation of an enterprise purchases materials and machines and employs persons, makes products and sells them in the market. Like a human being, an organism learns, judges and behaves by using its head, hands and feet: an organisation as enterprise judges, decides and behaves depending on the information collected by its managers. However, we must not overlook the fact that the enterprise receives the influence of the cultural structure and the economic process. This is because the members of an enterprise are individual persons whose behaviour patterns or value systems are conditioned by the cultural structure of their time and their country, and because the decisions of the managers of the enterprise are normally made after considering other competitive enterprises, along with the industrial tendency of both the domestic and foreign economic situations.

These three factors, namely the cultural structure, the economic process, and the internal and external organisation of the enterprise, are relatively independent of each other. But, each has some effect on the other factors. Therefore we can find the case where the first factor has a strong effect on the other two factors in a particular era, or the other case where the second or third factor has a strong influence on the others in another particular era. Therefore, we must analyse the mutual influences of the three factors not only from the historical aspect but also from international comparisons. The cultural structure has been studied in the field of sociology (inclusive of the study of religion, law etc.,), the economic process in economics, and the organisation of the enterprise in management science. Of course, we must take an interdisciplinary approach in order to discuss the transferability of management. The interrelationship of Nakagawa's three factors can be seen in Figures 1 and 2 with respect to different countries and their historical process.

The results of a Japan Management Association (Nippon Noritsu Kyokai) questionnaire

In 1982, the Japan Management Association sent out a questionnaire by post to 635 manufacturing companies on their production techniques and on the transferability of production systems. 238 companies (including 85 companies which have subsidiaries in foreign countries) gave responses. From their responses, three points concerning the transferability of management style will be introduced here(3).

The first point is the difference between the level of productivity of the mother company in Japan and the subsidiaries in foreign countries, which is shown below:

100% of the productivity of mother company in Japan	17.6%
Between 100% and 80%	41.2%
Between 80% - 60%	25.9%
Under 60%	11.8%
No answer	3.5%
Number of companies responding = 85	100.0%

Considering the area where the subsidiaries are located, this report explains that the productivity level of subsidiaries located in North America is very high and that over 80 per cent of all subsidiaries in this area attain 80 per cent of the productivity level of the Japanese mother company. But, the productivity level of the subsidiaries in the area of South-East Asia is conspicuously low. The reasons for this difference in productivity are shown as follows:

a.	quality of the workforce, for example the skill of local workers etc.	35 answers
b.	absenteeism	9 "
c.	character of the people of the country as regards diligence or will to work	8 "
d.	production equipment and process	8 "
e.	quality of raw materials and parts which are supplied	5 "
f.	ability of supervisors	2 "
g.	no answer	5
	Number of answers	74

Figure 3 explains the second point: how the production line is transferred to the foreign subsidiary. As shown in the figure, 30 per cent of 85 companies have transferred the same production line from the mother company to the local factories. But 54 per cent answered that the production line of the Japanese mother company could not be directly transferred but had to be improved, while the other 14 per cent answered that, 'A quite new production line had to be set up in the local factory'. Then what are the reasons why the production line had to be improved in the case of its transfer to the local factory? The reasons are shown below:

a.	to improve the negative points of the Japanese production line	5 answers
b.	differences in the quality or standard of parts which are supplied locally	4 "
c.	low levels of local skill and technology	8 "
d.	smaller scale of production system than that of the Japanese mother company	7 "
e.	differences in the standard or quality of products or differences in the market	5 "
f.	different local social, economic and legal systems	12 "
		41

The third point and the most interesting one here, is to what degree the production systems of the Japanese mother company are being introduced into the local factory. The Japan Management Association selected the following four factors as the specific aspects which show the introduction of the Japanese system, namely:

(1) the system of inspecting product quality within the production process
(2) suggestions schemes
(3) the system of multi-function workers and multi-process holding and,
(4) the system of small group activities.

Tables 1, 2 3 and 4 show the percentages and the absolute number of companies which have successfully or unsuccessfully introduced these systems in different manufacturing areas and in different countries and the degree of utilisation of manuals.

In general, 60 percent of the 85 companies with foreign subsidiaries have introduced the system of inspection of product quality within the production process. The suggestion system has been introduced in 51 per cent of the local factories, the system of multi-function workers and multi-process holding in 40 per cent, and the system of small group activities in 36 per cent of the subsidiaries.

Now the degree of success of each factor in the different

areas will be examined:

(1) The system inspecting product quality within the production process. From the point of view of the form of manufacturing, the successful cases are found more in the assembly line than in the case of the plant form. By area, 81 per cent of local factories in Korea and Taiwan have introduced this systems, and 60 per cent in North America and South-East Asia. Moreover, the percentage of successful cases in Korea and Taiwan is larger than the percentage of cases in North America and South-East Asia. In terms of the degree of utilisation of manuals, a high percentage of local factories that describe their manuals less concretely than in Japan have introduced this system. But we cannot find a relationship between the degree of utilisation of manuals and the percentage of successful cases for this system.

(2) Suggestion schemes. From the point of view of the form of manufacturing, the proportion of introduction and successful outcome of suggestion systems is higher in the assembly line than in the plant form. A high percentage of local factories in Korea, Taiwan, South-East Asia and North America have introduced this system but the successful cases can be found in Korea and Taiwan. Over 50 per cent of local factories in South America and Europe have said, 'We have no intention to introduce this system'. Concerning the degree of utilisation of manuals, as in the example above, this system has been introduced more in the factories which describe their manual less concretely than in Japan.

(3) The system of multi-function workers and multi-process holding. Concerning the introduction of this system into different manufacturing forms, we cannot find as much difference between the form of the assembly line and the plant form as can be found with the other three systems. By area, this system has been introduced into Asian countries to a great extent and Korea and Taiwan have introduced this system most successfully. With the degree of utilisation of manuals, we have found quite the opposite tendency compared with the other three systems. That is, local factories whose manuals are more detailed than those in Japan, or with the same degree of detail, can introduce this system successfully.

(4) System of small group activities. From the point of view of the form of manufacturing, small group activities have been introduced more in the assembly line than the plant form and

the proportion of successful cases that can be found is also higher in the assembly line. By area, these small group activities have been introduced positively in Asian countries such as Korea and Taiwan. In contrast, many local factories in South America, North America and Europe have no intention to introduce this system. Regarding the utilisation of manuals, a high percentage of local factories that do not describe their manuals so concretely have introduced this system. However, the more successful cases can be found in the factories whose manuals are more detailed than in Japanese factories.

Theoretical problems of the transferability of management style - from the aspect of the transfer of skills.

The expression 'Management Style' is ambiguous. In this paper the transferability of management style will be discussed from the aspect of the transfer of skills. The techniques used in an enterprise include not only the technique with which a worker operates a machine for production or for data processing but also the technique with which a manager can control workers in the process of purchasing, manufacturing, selling, financing, data processing, educational training and research and development etc. The former technique is called machine operation technique, which can be analysed as the relation between man and machine. The latter technique is called management technique, which can be analysed as the relation between man and man well as between man and machine, because the management of an enterprise has no meaning without the production of goods and services. Both techniques have effects on each other. Originally both techniques exist internally in manual work and are called 'skills'.

In the context of the historical economic development of different countries, the Industrial Revolution established the factory system in all countries, although the beginning of the era was different in different cases. One of the characteristics of the Industrial Revolution was the mechanisation of working tools, through which the dual phenomena of the transfer of skills occurred. The first phenomenon is the transfer of skills from workers to machinery. It means that the subjective value or individual skill of a skilled worker, who had a position of initiative at the workplace, decreased and that machinery took over the position of initiative in the workshop. For its result, the efficiency of work in the workshop mostly depends upon the efficiency of the machinery and the content of the worker's job becomes routine work. This phenomenon is called the mechanisation of work.

The second phenomenon is the transfer of skills from the workers to the managers. It means that the work in which the individual skilled worker so far been engaged could be divided into two kinds of work. One is independent manual work and the other is management work, by which each dependent task has to be coordinated and controlled and the job of coordination or control is carried out professionally by a manager or entrepreneur. This phenomenon is called the managerialisation of work(4).

When considering these phenomena, we must not overlook the fact that the managerialisation of work can be found in the mechanisation process of work and that at the same time the managerialisation of work will promote more mechanisation of work. F.W. Taylor, in his book 'Principles of Scientific Management', mainly discussed the managerialisation of work based on time and motion studies, while Henry Ford, with his belt conveyor system, simultaneously promoted the mechanisation of work and the managerialisation of work based on the standardisation of work and of the parts to be used on the assembly line. Furthermore, the remarkable development of computer technology since the Second World War has brought a third transfer of skills. It is the mechanisation of the clerical work originally needed for management work.

If we analyse these phenomena from the standpoint of a worker who had his own individual skills, it means that his position or rank at the workplace is degraded in terms of skill(5). In other words, it means that his skills are transferred to the machinery or managers on the one hand and that his personality is impoverished or depersonalised (Entindividualisierung) on the other hand(6). Therefore skilled workers or craft unions were against the diffusion of machines or the Taylor system in the past. Of course, the mechanisation of work also made unskilled workers capable of performing tasks by using machines which they could not do in the past.

According to my opinion, the mechanisation of work (including clerical work) and the managerialisation of work depend upon each other, but their interdependency is different in each country. Occasionally the mechanisation of work (including clerical work) may develop independently of the mangerialisation of work because the mechanisation of work is connected with the relation between man and machine, whereas the managerialisation of work is mainly connected with the relation between man (manager) and man (worker), although it is also connected with the relation of man andmachine. For example, the system of multi-function workers and multi-process holding is directly connected with the relation of man and machine, while Japanese employment systems such as the lifetime employment system, the system of wage increases and promotion based on years of service and the periodical hiring system, are not directly connected with the relation of man and machine but just with the relation between man and man.

As an inherent mechanism to operate a machine exists, the operating method for the machine can easily be standardised by utilising a manual. The worker may soon learn how to operate it after some training. On the other hand, the technique of managing man (workers) requires much knowledge on the part of a manager and to standardise operations and utilise the manual is more difficult in this case. In other words, the degree of the transfer of skills from workers to managers depends much more upon the management philosophy of the enterprise, the loyalty of workers and the cultural structure of the country as the behaviour patterns or the value system of the individual person. Therefore the degree of standardisation or utilisation of manuals for management work may differ from enterprise to enterprise, especially from sector to sector or from one form of manufacturing to another, and from country to country.

If the above hypothesis is correct, we can say that it is not so difficult to transfer machines and their operating techniques from one country to another, although it depends upon the technical level (the quality of workers, the techniques related to the operating and maintenance of the machine etc.,) and the economic, social and legal conditions of the country. In this type of transfer the worker can operate the machine by learning and having training according to the manual. By comparison, the transfer of management techniques from one country to another do not seem to be smooth enough, because the transfer of skill is from man to man, which is conspicuously different from country to country.

The fact that the American system of job descriptions could not fit Japanese enterprise culture just before the beginning of high economic growth, supports this hypothesis. Namely, at the beginning of the 1950s Japanese employers tried to introduce the American management system whereby the scope and content of the jobs (authority and responsibility) of managers and workers were clearly defined. However, Japanese managers came to know that it was quite impossible to define the content or scope of an administrative job objectively, even when authority was formally assigned to it as far as possible, and that it was unrealistic to expect such a change within the context of such Japanese organisational and personnel practices as the lifetime employment system, the seniority system and the group decision-making system(7).

Clarification of the job and its authority in particular was contrary to the traditional Ringi system. For this reason, the American system could not be directly introduced but had to be modified with the modernisation of the Ringi system. That is, the content and scope of the job is clarified by groups, by sections and by departments. In addition, the modern American general staff system was also introduced in the process of modernising the Ringi system(8).

In general, techniques like hardware are relatively easy to transfer to other countries, while techniques like software will be difficult. As every country has its own cultural structure, social and economic situation, legal conditions, technical levels and management organisation, the degree of transferability of machines on the one hand and of management techniques on the other will be quite different. But the transfer of management style can be promoted gradually by some modifications to it, in order to fit into a country's own management style, because the internationalisation of business depends on mutual understanding in all the various fields of culture, economy, education, law and technology etc., between the different countries.

Notes

(1) K. Nakagawa. Japanese Management Style, (in Japanese), Japan Broadcast Association, Tokyo 1981. pp.11-26.

(2) Nakagawa, op.cit., pp.19-22 'Gerschenkron, Alexander. Economic Backwardness in Historical Perspective', in: The Progress of Underdeveloped Areas, (ed). B.F. Hoselitz, 1951.

(3) Japan Management Association. (Nippon Noritsu Kyokai) Research Report on the Transferability of Japanese Management Style to Foreign Countries, (in Japanese) Tokyo, 1982, pp.87-115.

(4) S. Mori, The Basic Theory of Management, (in Japanese) Tokyo 1977, pp.114-115, The Theory of Business Administration, (in Japanese) Tokyo 1977, p.397.

(5) H. Braverman. Labour and Monopoly. The Degradation of Work in the Twentieth Century, Monthly Review Press, 1974.

(6) E. Gutenberg. Grundlagen der Betriebswirtschaftslehre, 18 Auflage 1971, p.238.

(7) K. Noda 'Big Business Organisation', in: Modern Japanese Organisation and Decision-Making, (ed). Ezra, F. Vogel, University of California 1975, p.138.

(8) Y. Takahashi. 'Japanese Management Style. Historical analysis and International Comparison', (in German), Research Paper No. 3 of the Institute of Business Research, Chuo University, Tokyo, 1984, pp.57-64.

Table 1 Quality inspection within the process

	Population parameter	Successful	Unsuccessful	No intention to introduce	No answer
Total (per cent)	100.0	47.1	12.9	22.4	17.6
	85	40	11	19	15
Manufacturing form					
Plant form	100.0	30.0	15.0	25.0	30.0
	20	6	3	5	6
Assembly line	100.0	50.0	16.7	23.3	10.0
	30	15	5	7	3
Other	100.0	51.5	9.1	21.2	18.2
	33	17	3	7	6
No answer	100.0	100.0	-	-	-
	2	2	-	-	-
Local factory location					
North America	100.0	50.0	10.0	30.0	10.0
	10	5	1	3	1
South America	100.0	12.5	12.5	62.5	12.5
	8	1	1	5	1
Korea/Taiwan	100.0	56.3	25.0	12.5	6.3
	16	9	4	2	1
South-East Asia	100.0	53.8	7.7	17.9	20.5
	39	21	3	7	8
Europe	100.0	40.0	-	40.0	20.0
	5	2	-	2	1
Australia	100.0	50.0	-	-	50.0
	2	1	-	-	1
Middle and Near East	100.0	-	-	-	100.0
	1	-	-	-	1
Other	100.0	25.0	50.0	-	25.0
	4	1	2	-	1

(Table continued over page)

Table 1 (continued)

	Population parameter	Quality inspection within the process: Successful	Unsuccessful	No intention to introduce	No answer
Degree of utilisation of manuals					
More concretely than Japanese	100.0	41.9	12.9	22.6	22.6
	31	13	4	7	7
Same as Japanese	100.0	53.6	10.7	17.9	17.9
	28	15	3	5	5
Not so concretely as Japanese	100.0	54.5	18.2	27.3	-
	11	6	2	3	-
Not defined	100.0	46.2	15.4	30.8	7.7
	13	6	2	4	1
No answer	100.0	-	-	-	100.0
	2	-	-	-	2

Source: Japan Management Association, ibid. p.107

Table 2 Introduction of suggestion schemes

	Population parameter	Successful	Unsuccessful	No intention to introduce	No answer
Total (per cent)	100.0	30.6	20.0	34.1	15.3
	85	40	17	29	13
Manufacturing form					
Plant form	100.0	20.0	25.0	35.0	20.0
	20	4	5	7	4
Assembly line	100.0	33.3	20.0	30.0	16.7
	30	10	6	9	5
Other	100.0	30.3	18.2	39.4	12.1
	33	10	6	13	4
No answer	100.0	100.0	-	-	-
	2	2	-	-	-
Local factory location					
North America	100.0	30.0	30.0	30.0	10.0
	10	3	3	3	1
South America	100.0	25.0	12.5	50.0	12.5
	8	2	1	4	1
Korea/Taiwan	100.0	43.8	12.5	25.0	18.8
	16	7	2	4	3
South-East Asia	100.0	28.2	25.6	30.8	15.4
	39	11	10	12	6
Europe	100.0	20.0	-	60.0	20.0
	5	1	-	3	1
Australia	100.0	50.0	50.0	-	-
	2	1	1	-	-
Middle and Near East	100.0	100.0	-	-	-
	1	1	-	-	-
Other	100.0	-	-	75.0	25.0
	4	-	-	3	1

(Table continued over page)

Table 2 (continued)

		Suggestion schemes			
	Population parameter	Successful	Unsuccessful	No intention to introduce	No answer
Degree of utilisation of manuals					
More concretely than Japanese	100.0	25.8	22.6	32.3	19.4
	31	8	7	10	6
Same as Japanese	100.0	42.9	10.7	39.3	7.1
	28	12	3	11	2
Not so concretely as Japanese	100.0	45.5	27.3	27.3	-
	11	5	3	3	-
Not defined	100.0	7.7	30.8	38.5	23.1
	13	1	4	5	3
No answer	100.0	-	-	-	100.0
	2	-	-	-	2

Source: Japan Management Association, ibid. p.106

Table 3 System of multi-function workers and multi-process holding

	Population parameter	Successful	Unsuccessful	No intention to introduce	No answer
Total (per cent)	100.0	21.2	18.8	38.8	21.2
	85	18	16	33	18
Manufacturing form					
Plant form	100.0	10.0	20.0	35.0	35.0
	20	2	4	7	7
Assembly line	100.0	20.0	23.3	40.0	16.7
	30	6	7	12	5
Other	100.0	27.3	12.1	42.4	18.2
	33	9	4	14	6
No answer	100.0	50.0	50.0	-	-
	2	1	1	-	-
Local factory location					
North America	100.0	20.0	10.0	60.0	10.0
	10	2	1	6	1
South America	100.0	-	12.5	75.0	12.5
	8	-	1	6	1
Korea/Taiwan	100.0	37.5	18.8	25.0	18.8
	16	6	3	4	3
South-East Asia	100.0	17.9	20.5	35.9	25.6
	39	7	8	14	10
Europe	100.0	40.0	-	40.0	20.0
	5	2	-	2	1
Australia	100.0	50.0	50.0	-	-
	2	1	1	-	-
Middle and Near East	100.0	-	-	-	100.0
	1	-	-	-	1
Other	100.0	-	50.0	25.0	25.0
	4	-	2	1	1

(Table continued over page)

Table 3 (continued)

	Multi-function workers				
	Population parameter	Successful	Unsuccessful	No intention to introduce	No answer
Degree of utilisation of manuals					
More concretely than Japanese	100.0	25.8	19.4	32.3	22.6
	31	8	7	10	6
Same as Japanese	100.0	28.6	7.1	42.9	21.4
	28	8	2	12	6
Not so concretely as Japanese	100.0	9.1	45.5	45.5	-
	11	1	5	5	-
Not defined	100.0	7.7	23.1	46.2	23.1
	13	1	3	6	3
No answer	100.0	-	-	-	100.0
	2	-	-	-	2

Source: Japan Management Association, ibid. p.108

Table 4 Introduction of small group activities

	Population parameter	Successful	Unsuccessful	No intention to introduce	No answer
Total	100.0	18.8	17.6	43.5	20.0
	85	16	15	37	17
Manufacturing form					
Plant form	100.0	5.0	15.0	55.0	25.0
	20	1	3	11	5
Assembly line	100.0	26.7	13.3	36.7	23.3
	30	8	4	11	7
Other	100.0	21.2	21.2	45.5	12.1
	33	7	7	15	4
No answer	100.0	-	50.0	-	50.0
	2	-	1	-	1
Local factory location					
North America	100.0	30.0	-	60.0	10.0
	10	3	-	6	1
South America	100.0	-	12.5	75.0	12.5
	8	-	1	6	1
Korea/Taiwan	100.0	37.5	12.5	37.5	12.5
	16	6	2	6	2
South-East Asia	100.0	15.4	28.2	33.3	23.1
	39	6	11	13	9
Europe	100.0	-	-	60.0	40.0
	5	-	-	3	2
Australia	100.0	-	50.0	-	50.0
	2	-	1	-	1
Middle and Near East	100.0	100.0	-	-	-
	1	1	-	-	-
Other	100.0	-	-	75.0	25.0
	4	-	-	3	1

(Table continued over page)

Table 4 (continued)

	Multi-function workers				
	Population parameter	Successful	Unsuccessful	No intention to introduce	No answer
Degree of utilisation of manuals					
More concretely than Japanese	100.0	22.6	6.5	41.9	29.0
	31	7	2	13	9
Same as Japanese	100.0	17.9	17.9	53.6	10.7
	28	5	5	15	3
Not so concretely as Japanese	100.0	27.3	36.4	36.4	-
	11	3	4	4	-
Not defined	100.0	7.7	30.8	38.5	23.1
	13	1	4	5	3
No answer	100.0	-	-	-	100.0
	2	-	-	-	2

Source: Japan Management Association, ibid. p.104

Figure 1 Historical and International Comparison of three factors

Period	Cultural structure	Company organisation	Economic process
Meija Era 1868		Ringi system First labour unions	Start of industrialisation
1919	Suppression of unions	Lifetime employment Seniority wage system Periodical hiring	From external labour market to internal labour market
1945	Women's rights Democratic union law Increase in small families Changing attitudes of young. Ageing population	American management introduced (Ringi system modified) Seniority wage system modified Lifetime employment only in large companies Increase in irregular employees	Dissolution of zaibatsu (1) First stage of high economic growth - 1958 (2) Second stage of high economic growth - 1965 Oil shock - 1972 (3)
Japan			
USA			
Europe			
Asia			
Countries / Factors	Cultural structure	Company organisation	Economic process

(1) Approximately 40 per cent of all employees belong to the primary sector
(2) Increasing numbers of employees in secondary sector
(3) Approximately 50 per cent of all employees belong to the tertiary sector

Figure 2 International comparison of value systems and organisation

Japan	Group spirit Confucianism	. indefinite scope of job . group decision (bottom	. stock holding by corporation . strong competition between groups and group enterprises
	Weak social class	. enterprise union	. dual structure of the economy
U.S.A.	Individualism	. definite scope of job	. stock holding by institutional investors
	States of many peoples Less rigid social class	. top down decision . industrial union	. strong competition between individuals
Europe	Individualism/rigid social class		
W. Germany	Protestantism	. definite scope of job . top down decision	. stockholding by family
France	Catholicism	. industrial union	. not so strong competition between enterprises as in USA and Japan
UK	Puritanism	. craft union	. European community
Asia (Korea, Taiwan, South-East Asia)			
Countries three factors	Cultural structure (sociology)	Organisation of the enterprise (management science)	Economic process (economics)

Figure 3 How are Japanese production techniques transferred to foreign subsidiaries?

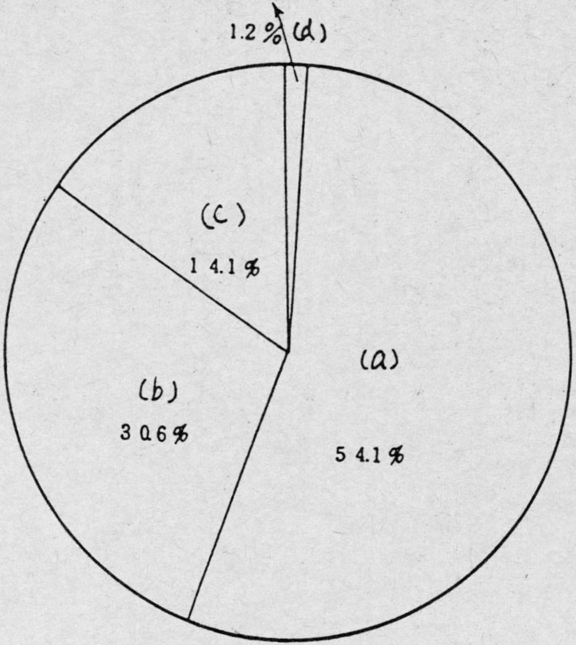

N = 85

(a)	modification of the Japanese production line	(54.11%)
(b)	same production line as Japanese mother company	(30.6%)
(c)	quite new production line	(14.1%)
(d)	no answer	(1.2%)

THE RECRUITMENT, SELECTION AND JOB SATISFACTION OF EXPATRIATE MANAGERS IN JAPANESE AND GERMAN MULTI-NATIONAL CORPORATIONS

B. Kumar and H. Steinmann
University of Erlangen-Nuremberg

This study was supported by the Hans-Frisch-Stiftung (Nuremberg) to whom we would like to express our gratitude.

Introduction

In recent years Japanese companies have been steadily substituting and complementing their export activities with local production and/or local trading subsidiaries abroad. In the wake of this development an increasing number of Japanese expatriate managers is being sent overseas, especially since Japanese firms seem to be quite conservative with respect to assigning local managers to comparable jobs in their foreign subsidiaries(1).

According to White(2), one factor that has been responsible for explaining the achievement of Japanese firms is their range of practices and policies concerning human resource management. This seems to be also in line with Misumi and Peterson(3), who attribute part of Japan's recent success to good leadership, which can be seen as a special aspect of personnel management. So we assume that one comparative advantage Japanese multinational corporations (MNCs) may have over international companies of other nationalities lies in the **culturally specific** manner they assign parent company managers to overseas positions. In the following paper an attempt is made to uncover and explain similarities and dissimilarities between Japanese and German MNCs in the way they handle expatriate administration, especially the problem of recruitment and selection of home company managers for foreign assignment. The comparative approach may enable us to identify Japanese strengths and weaknesses more clearly and to understand their management system better.

The comparative framework

A meaningful analysis and informative discussion of the topic must recognise the importance of culture in management. A comparative study of recruitment and selection practices in Japanese and German MNCs will have to be based on the effects of culture on these two aspects of expatriate management. Our approach to the investigation will be, first, to identify similarities and dissimilarities between German and Japanese MNCs as ascertained in our empirical findings. Next, each aspect will be evaluated in the light of its cultural underpinnings and then compared with reference to the two nationalities. For this purpose we need a specification of the **relevant** cultural characteristics pertaining to Japan and Germany.

Several concepts have been proposed in the pertinent literature for this type of characterisation of culture(4). We choose to elaborate our findings along the cultural dimensions advanced by Hofstede(5) for cross-cultural management research(6):

(1) individualism-collectivism
(2) power-distance
(3) uncertainty avoidance, and
(4) masculinity-feminity.

Since this concept is meant to be applied to all management functions, not all four dimensions need necessarily be applicable to the recruitment and selection of expatriates. In any case, in the following only some selected relationships between culture and each of the two aspects of expatriate administration can be exemplified in order to keep within the given range of this paper.

Questionnaire and sample

The findings presented in this paper are based on two studies undertaken by the authors. The first one was conducted in 1982/83 and involved a questionnaire survey of 135 Japanese expatriate managers assigned to positions in 37 subsidiaries of Japanese multinational companies in Germany. The second study in 1984/85 took the opposite view and was based on a questionnaire survey of 101 German expatriate executives in Japan. The questions posed in both questionnaires were more or less the same, pertaining to issues of strategic and personnel management, including aspects of expatriate administration. For comprehension purposes, the questionnaires were in the respective native language of the respondents.

Regarding their personal and organisational characteristics, the Japanese and German respondents were similar in most respects, with little difference in some features. To name a few important characteristics: in both cases the larger percentage of respondents belonged to firms in the industrial sector, for example, electrical and mechanical. Somewhat more Japanese expatriates were attached to firms in the service sector (banking, insurance) than German respondents. In both cases about half of the responding managers were involved with general management either as President/Chairman or as Vice-President/General Manager. The rest of the respondents of both nationalities were assigned to different functional areas (marketing, production) in the rank of Director or Manager.

By far the majority of the respondents of both nationalities represented firms which were classified as large multinational corporations; in other words, the parent companies in Japan and Germany employed more than a thousand employees. The subsidiaries in Germany and Japan were in both cases much smaller with around 100-200 employees on the average. These subsidiaries in both cases were considered by most of the respondents to be an important part of the total overseas operations of the respective companies.

Regarding some personal characteristics, in both cases the large majority (over 90 per cent) of the responding expatriates were married, and had their spouse and children accompany them to Germany or Japan respectively. The Japanese expatriates were somewhat younger than their German counterparts, the average age being around 40 compared to 43 years in the latter case. With the organisational and personal characteristics of the Japanese and German respondents being by and large similar, we can neglect any differentiating influence on that account and can assume that any dissimilarity found between the two nationalities will be mainly due to cultural differences.

Recruitment

The findings

Recruitment in the questionnaires was defined and interpreted as the activity carried out **initially** in order to take up or fill a job abroad. Our results disclose that both Japanese and German expatriate managers were recruited for their representative assignments in three different ways. As shown in Table 1, the majority of managers of both nationalities had initially not been active by themselves, but had been told more or less unexpectedly by the company to take up a position abroad.

Only a relatively small portion of the respondents stated to have been active and to have sought a foreign assignment by themselves and a still smaller number of German respondents mentioned that their foreign posting had been mutually planned by the company and themselves on a long-term basis.

The results can be interpreted in two ways. They show a certain **similarity** between the Japanese and German expatriates in the sense that within each nationality the larger percentage of respondents had actually not sought a foreign posting on their own, but had been (unexpectedly) approached by the company to take up an overseas assignment. The **difference**, however, becomes apparent when the extent of each type of recruitment is compared with each other between the nationalities: far more Japanese had taken up their posting on the company's orders than had German managers. Moreover, twice as many of the German respondents had initiated the assignment by themselves or had it planned on a longer term basis. It is interesting to note that in none of the two nationality categories were there any really significant differences in the results according to the aforementioned personal and organisational characteristics of the respondents. A slight trend was noticeable in both groups along the position hierarchy of the managers, in the sense that recruitment on a manager's own initiative was slightly more pronounced among expatriates in the higher echelons than in the lower positions. Since the age of respondents correlated with the position hierarchy in both groups, one might also suggest a slight relationship between the former and recruitment practice.

Discussion

Looking at the three listed recruitment methods closely, one discovers that the essential difference between them rests basically on two factors; on the amount of uncertainty or risk respectively connected with each alternative for the company as well as the expatriate. For instance, at one end of the scale planned recruitment helps to reduce risk and uncertainty for expatriates, in as much as their personal development for the future is mapped out. The posting abroad does not come as a surprise and the manager is prepared for it. The advantage for the company lies in the fact that the risk of a sudden shortage of personnel (qualified) for recruitment is lowered. At the other extreme, the element of uncertainty is high when managers do not themselves actively explore the possibility of a posting abroad, but are approached by the company at rather short notice to take up an overseas assignment.

Secondly, the difference between the three recruitment methods pertains to the question as to how much the manager is **personally involved** in the process. When recruitment for a foreign assignment is mutually planned, then the self-interest of the potential expatriate is integrated into the affairs of the company in the form of career planning. On the other hand, when managers are told to take up a foreign assignment at short notice, then their individual needs are not apparently given much attention in comparison with the firm's interests.

This analysis makes clear that both these factors are two inherent (cultural) prerequisites of recruitment practice(7). An analysis of our findings regarding the dissimilarities between Japanese and German MNCs in this question must, therefore, consider the culturally supported differences of view between the two nationalities towards uncertainty and risk as well as self-interest and individual needs and their influence on recruitment. For this purpose we refer to Hofstede's (1983) concept of culture and identity as correspondingly relevant cultural dimensions 'uncertainty avoidance' and 'individualism-collectivism'.

In Hofstede's own words, 'The fundamental issue involved in 'uncertainty-avoidance' is how society deals with the fact that time runs only one way... that we have to live with uncertainty because the future is unknown and always will be. Some societies socialise their members into accepting this uncertainty and not becoming upset by it. They will take risks rather easily... Other societies socialise their people into trying to beat the future... In those societies there will be a higher level of anxiety in people... Such societies also have institutions that try to create security and avoid risk ...'

According to Hofstede's cultural map (Figure 1), Germany, as compared to many countries, has a high uncertainty - avoidance score which, however, is considerably lower than that of Japan. This means that German firms will lay more emphasis on uncertainty and risk avoidance in management than comparable US companies by, for instance, systematically planning recruitment and foreign assignment to a greater extent. This theoretical difference seems absolutely plausible when one takes into account how many long-term obligations German firms have in practice towards employees, as compared to ad hoc personnel practices ('hire and fire') in most US companies(8).

By the same token, Japanese firms on the other hand, will lay even greater importance on risk avoidance practices. But as our findings show, in no single case were Japanese expatriates recruited on the basis of career planning, which in the German case was considered to be congenial for reducing uncertainty. The explanation for this seeming contradiction lies in the fact that in Japanese firms other means of personnel recruitment for postings in and outside the country exist, by which a greater reduction of risk for both employer and employee is possible. One such system is surely the Japanese life-long employment scheme (Shushin-

Koyo). According to Baliga and Jaeger(9), this concept has a tremendous **stabilising** effect on the total system and organisational culture. Although the roots of life-long employment in Japanese firms go back to the Taisho era of 1912-26(10), it became popular only in the post-war period as an outcome of felt insecurity due to severe labour conflicts and bad economic conditions(11). Even though restricted mainly to executives in large corporations and to college-leavers, this aspect of personnel administration is one of the unique dimensions of Japanese management, and is even considered by some to be one of its main strengths. It offers managers fixed employment until retirement age, job training throughout their careers and regular promotion on the basis of seniority(12). With this type of security offered, firms in return require executives to be highly motivated and committed to the organisation's policies, like sudden and frequent transfers within and outside the country. And, indeed, because executives in this system do not fear change, loyalty is high(13). An indication of this can be seen in our findings that most Japanese expatriates had come to Germany because they had been told to do so by their respective companies(14). In this system, long-term recruitment policies like manpower and career planning of the kind used in German enterprises to ward off obstructive behaviour when change (risk, insecurity) is contemplated will have a low priority.

The other relevant cultural dimension underlying recruitment for foreign postings is 'individualism-collectivism'. According to Hofstede, the fundamental issue involved here is, 'The relation between and individual and his or her fellow individuals. At one end of the scale we find societies in which the ties between individuals are very loose. Everybody is supposed to look after his or her own self-interest. At the other end of the scale we find societies in which the ties between individuals are very tight. People are born into collectiveness or in-groups... In exchange, the in-group will protect them when they are in trouble'.

The fact that German shows a higher individualism score than Japan, which on the other hand has a higher collectivism rating (Figure 2), may explain our findings with respect to the difference between the recruiting practices ot the two nationalities. The stronger tendency and the greater extent to which their recruitment was planned (as compared to Japanese expatriates) is compatible with the greater importance of individual needs in the German culture. From the point of view of motivation, the best participation and long-term commitment of managers in the organisation is integrated into recruitment requirements in the form of personal initiative and career planning in which individual development is set out with regard to factors like pay, responsibility etc. Should individual need satisfaction in this respect be missing, then managers are liable to leave the organisation. In return, managers accept the fact that should their individual achievements not be in line with organisation requirements they could be asked to leave and the firm would recruit new members. In this respect, American managers - in accordance with Hofstede's individualism score for the USA (Figure 2) - show even stronger individualistic attitudes which, for instance, result in a lower committment of personnel to the company, as compared to German managers who, for instance, are more reluctant to leave their employer in exchange for another(15).

On the other hand, the high collectivism score for Japan (Figure 2) indicates that in this society group needs predominate over individual interests. So with respect to recruitment, Japanese managers wil seldom be active themselves but will rather react to company interests, as our findings also suggest.

Keeping back personal aspirations in favour of apprehending group interest is also compatible with the system of life-long employment as described earlier. Sociologists point out that looking at the firm as one family (Kigyo-ikkei) and the spread of life-time employment have coincided with the replacement of the joint family by many small nuclear families in Japanese society(16). Corporate paternalism and life-time employment meet the group needs of Japanese society. As Yang(17) points out, 'Life-time employment works best in (Japanese) society where the subordination of an individual's private life to the larger group is necessary and honourable'. So this again explains why Japanese expatriates were less active about being recruited than their German colleagues. Moreover, because personal careers are more or less fixed in the Japanese life-long employment system, it is also fairly clear why there were no cases among the Japanese expatriates where foreign assignments were pre-planned.

While the above analysis explains the differences in recruitment of Japanese and German expatriates and also why most of the former were not active by themselves, the question still remains why within the German group a larger number of managers was passive and not exposed to career planning, although the cultural underpinnings of recruitment do seem to suggest the opposite. For one, this behaviour could be interpreted as a sign of bad practice, in the sense that many German firms (more than Japanese) are not sensitive to cultural influences and have simply neglected manpower planning(17). But on the other hand, it could also be an indication that firms intentionally keep recruitment for foreign assignments open and unplanned in order to remain flexible and to be able to react as opportunities appear. This approach -which incidentally appears to be more acceptable to German firms than to Japanese because of uncertainty-avoidance - would also encourage flexibility and the development of broad capabilities among managers, in other words of qualifications badly needed on foreign assignments(18).

Selection

The findings

In both our questionnaires an attempt was made to find out what the selection criteria were on whose basis expatriate managers in both nationality groups had been chosen for their respective assignments in Germany and Japan. Naturally, selection criteria will basically depend upon the type of job the person is expected to do. Now, expatriate executives can of course be assigned to various functional areas, and their job descriptions will vary accordingly. However, one can assume that all expatriate managers will also have some common job requirements in accordance with the general character of the foreign assignment within the activity of the multinational enterprise. In fact these special job requirements represent the logic for assigning parent company staff instead of local nationals to managerial positions in foreign subsidiaries. These positional needs are deduced from the general characteristics of the multinational activity of firms and are basically twofold: the transfer of know-how and resources from the parent company to the subsidiaries, and the coordination and integration of the subsidiaries' activity within the global strategy of the multinational corporation(19).

Our findings confirm these points. In Table 2 the important reasons in each group for expatriate assignment as seen by the groups themselves are listed. It is interesting to note that the rank order of both main motives is interchanged between the two nationality groups: for German expatriates in Japan the requirement of the coordination and integration of subsidiary activities into the global strategy was more important than the transfer of know-how; for Japanese expatriates in Germany it was the other way around. Besides these two main reasons some other general motives were also listed which are not discussed here.

Turning now to the selection criteria (Table 3) we find that the important items among them by and large coincide with the aforementioned job requirements: good knowledge of the parent company for transferring parent company resources, combined with ability in the integration of the subsidiary's activity into the global strategy ranked first and second among the Japanese and Germans respectively. The ability to adapt transferred know-how to the host country environment rated second in the Japanese group and was one rank higher than among the German respondents, which coincides with the higher emphasis the former seems to lay on the job requirements of expatriates concerning the training of local personnel (see Table 2). So regarding the application of selection criteria derived from the special job requirements of multinational activity there appears at the aggregate level to be more similarity than dissimilarity between the two nationality groups.

The only striking dissimilarity in importance concerns a more **general** trait: the item 'preparedness/ability to take over responsibility' was the most important selection criterion among German expatriates, and only third in the Japanese group. Other (dis-) similarities worth mentioning at the aggregate level are that both groups perceived relatively little or no importance in the willingness or consent of the wife and family to accompany the expatriate as a selection criterion; however, more consideration was given to it among German managers. And what is perhaps more surprising, the item 'knowledge of the native language of the host-country' ranked at the bottom of the ladder among both nationalities.

Viewing the results on a disaggregate basis, some dissimilarities become apparent when the age and position of respondents and the size of firm (parent company and subsidiary) are taken into account as differentiating factors. In the Japanese group the importance of all the selection criteria mentioned rose with the age of expatriates, with the exception of the item 'ability to adapt knowledge' which related inversely with position in the hierarchy (and age, considering the positive relationship between these two personal characteristics). Among the German respondents, only the importance of the item 'preparedness to take over responsibility' showed any significant relationship to the age of respondents. And finally, the importance of the items 'language knowledge' and 'willingness of spouse to accompany expatriate' was higher among Japanese belonging to smaller firms; in the German group, leadership ability scored higher in large companies.

Discussion

The most important dissimilarity between the selection practices for German and Japanese expatriates was found in the different emphasis laid on the trait 'preparedness/ability to take over responsibility'. As pointed out earlier, this factor is a general job characteristic and by nature applicable to all managerial positions irrespective of the particular function attached to them. The fact that this criterion ranked first in the choice of German expatriates seems to be connected with some underlying cultural dimensions.

Keeping within Hofstede's concept of culture, one of the pertinent influences seems to come from 'individualism' in German society, as described earlier. In short, the dominance of individual interests over group needs is a legitimation for self-fulfillment, which on its part is considered to be the utmost in individual need satisfaction in terms of motivation theory (Maslow, Herzberg). Self-fulfillment or self-actualisation in turn is basically connected with individual autonomy and its complementary element of personal responsibility for the actions individuals are free to take. In Western societies like Germany social organisations make use of these value expectations by defining positions on clear lines of competence by which individual responsibility can be identified. Subsequently, the emphasis on ability and the preparedness of candidates to bear responsibility as a selection criterion is seen by organisations as a success factor in personnel management. Especially in positions in foreign subsidiaries it is important to emphasise authority and responsibility mainly for two reasons: firstly, to make foreign jobs attractive to potential expatriates, since studies show that German managers are not particularly keen to take up appointments abroad(20). Secondly, the division of work and the degree of specialisation in foreign subsidiaries are generally less than in the German parent companies, and consequently more responsibility is attached to each position(21).

Turning now to the Japanese case we find that the relevant cultural variable 'individualism' has a much lower score in Japan, and 'collectivism' a much higher rating than in Germany (Figure 2). Indeed, there are few societal aspects in Japan that are so prominent and affect management so affirmatively as the groupism which is ascribed to this cultural dimension. As Marsland and Beer observe, Japanese individuals describe themselves first as members of a group, and then describe their position and role within that group. No Japanese feels that interdependence is better (or worse) than independence. Interdependence is a fact of nature, and harmonic interdependence is prized.

This holistic view of society affects behaviour in organisations. According to Yang, the functions that different members of an organisation in Japan perform are not specifically singled out. The contribution of each member is not distinguised from the performance of the whole. In such a situation group performance means more than individual achievement and self-actualisation. In compliance with this, collective decision-making relying on verbal and non-verbal communication prevails (Ringisho and Nemawashi)(22).

From this cultural underpinning and characteristic of management it is easy to see that the typical structural arrangement of the Japanese organisation fosters a form of authority and responsibility different from that found in Germany. As DeFrank et al. point out(23), the basic concern in the Japanese firm is not to determine clear lines of authority by which individual responsibility can be pinned on each specific manager. Rather, the overriding principle or organisation is harmony (Wa). And the important characteristic required of the manager is that he be a good member of the group and promote togetherness, which helps raise the morale and normally, in Yang's view, the productivity of the company's employees.

In this cultural context our finding is plausible that the ability and preparedness of Japanese expatriates to shoulder responsibility does not have so much priority as a selection criterion as was the case with German expatriates. It also explains why among the latter the importance of this particular characteristic rose with the position in the hierarchy and age of the respondents. Decision-making in Western enterprises is essentially a 'top-down' process, where defined lines of individual authority and responsibility gain importance with seniority. On the other hand, in the Japanese group the importance of all the applied selection criteria rose with the age and position in the hierarchy of respondents, which indicates that senior Japanese executives more than their German colleagues are required to possess a mix of different qualifications at a higher aspiration level. Evidently, this fosters the capabilities of the senior Japanese managers in performing their main job of establishing harmony (Wa) in the firm. As DeFrank et al. observe, Wa requires a voice, and the Japanese CEO is this voice: 'His responsibility is not to come up with innovative ideas that project the company into the future, but to find the way to sustain the present harmony within the organisation'.

Some differences in job satisfaction

The general picture of need fulfillment

The succes of foreign assignments can be interpreted in different ways(24). In our study the perceived job satisfaction of expatriate personnel was considered as an indicator of expatriate performance(25). We measured job satisfaction in terms of Porter's need deficiency concept along Maslow's categories of need fulfillment(26).

From Table 4 it can be seen that there are basic dissimilarities in job satisfaction. Among the German expatriates in Japan status needs were satisfied best and social needs the worst.

Interestingly, a relatively high deficiency in the satisfaction of self-actualisation needs can be noted among the German expatriates. This result compares unfavourably with the score in the Japanese group, who indeed experienced the highest need satisfaction with respect to self-actualisation. Our findings show that this discrepancy between the two nationalities is mainly accountable to the different aspiration levels of the expatriates: German expatriates had higher expectations regarding self-fulfillment in the job than their Japanese colleagues. This is compatible with the difference in the culturally based motivation of the expatriate as discussed previously.

The highest job dissatisfaction among the Japanese expatriates was experienced with respect to fulfillment of status needs. A possible explanation may be that a foreign assignment upsets the established pattern of group interrelations in which the Japanese expatriate is embedded at home. And because Japanese see all interrelations in terms of hierarchy(27) a disruption of status systems and, moreover, a loss of esteem may be felt in connection with a foreign assignment.

Relationship to recruitment and selection

In this section we hypothesise that the way expatriates are recruited and selected for a foreign assignment will affect their job satisfaction in their respective positions(28). After looking at the general picture and the practice followed in assigning German and Japanese expatriates we can expect some differences. Our findings show the following results:

Japanese expatriates who had been recruited for assignment in Germany on their own initiative (Table 1) showed higher fulfillment of social needs than their colleagues who had been told by the company to take up an assignment ($p \leq 0.05$).

German expatriates who had been recruited for assignment in Japan on their own initiative and on the basis of career planning showed higher fulfillment of security, status and self-actualisation needs than their colleagues who had been told by the company to take up an assignment ($p \leq 0.05$).

The results show that in both nationality groups recruitment practice does have repercussions on job satisfaction. The dissimilarity lies, however, in the extent. In the German group more aspects of job satisfaction were affected negatively than among the Japanese, when expatriates recruitment was not self initiated, and more or less enforced by the respective company. Ad hoc recruitment was felt to impinge on personal needs more by the German than by Japanese expatriates.

The explanation of the difference naturally lies in the cultural underpinnings of recruitment described previously. For instance, company-imposed recruitment in the case of Japanese expatriates meant being asked to transfer within a life-long employment system, to which the individual is obligated and committed and in which the path regarding personal development is more or less laid down up to retirement age. This and the phenomenon that individualism in Japanese culture is comparatively low seem to explain that even when the foreign assignment was not planned, no deficiency was felt regarding security and self-actualisation need fulfillment, as was the case among the German expatriates. On the other hand enforced recruitment among the Japanese does seem to have the effect that - as also mentioned before - their social bindings are disrupted, at least more than when they initiate a foreign assignment themselves. Subsequently, the perceived dissatisfaction of social needs is higher in the former case. The situation is exacerbated when recruitment is combined with parent company pressure on the subsidiary to absorb surplus personnel(29) who then find it hard to gain social acceptance there.

In comparison, unplanned recruitment for German expatriates meant that the role of the foreign assignment was not defined, or only vaguely defined, in the context of the individual's aspirations in respect of responsibility, competence and future development. Our results suggest that the actual situation experienced in the job evidently come up to expectations in this respect, thus leading to the perceived deficiency in security, self-actualisation and status needs.

The most important difference between the two nationalities concerning selection-related job satisafaction was found with respect to the job characteristic 'preparedness to take over responsibility'.

German expatriates who perceived greater importance in the criterion 'preparedness to take over responsibility' in connection with their selection for the job also expressed higher satisfaction of status and self-actualisation needs than managers who emphasised this job characteristic less ($p \leq 0.05$).

Among Japanese expatriates this selection criterion did not play an important role in job satisfaction.

In this result again the described difference in cultural values regarding the bearing of individual responsibility in both nationalities is reflected. Our results show that in comparison with the Japanese case, this selection criterion is definitely a success factor for German expatriate assignment in Japan.

Surprisingly, in both nationality groups knowledge of host

countries' language, which on the average rated low as a selection criterion, related positively to job satisfaction. German expatriates who rated the importance of this job characteristic higher in connection with their selection perceived better fulfillment of status needs than those colleagues who did not. Among the Japanese social needs were positively affected. As one can see, one and the same qualification is connected with a different gain according to nationality. The difference could lie in the different cultural background of the expatriates and the way they utilise this qualification; on the other hand, the difference could also be connected with the way local people of the respective host country who are recipients of this specific qualification respond to foreigners who have a knowledge of their native language.

Conclusion

Japan's sustained economic boom, the evident success achieved by so many Japanese enterprises and lately by multinational corporations have sparked interest in the nature of different aspects of Japanese management. In this paper an attempt has been made to compare the selection and recruitment of expatriate managers in Japanese enterprises with the practices followed in German MNCs. The underlying assumption in this problem obviously was that the selection and recruitment of the expatriates would be different, depending on the specific culture of the home country.

Our results by and large confirm this premise. On the other hand, there were also some similarities, especially regarding selection criteria in relation to the core tasks in MNCs. Apparently the nature of multinational activity and the specific job connected with it have an overriding effect which dominates the influence of culture on the selection of expatriates.

Our results moreover suggest that Japanese recruitment methods were more effective with regard to the perceived job satisfaction of the respective expatriates than the observed German practices. This is not necessarily a sign of superior Japanese management over German. Rather, as our findings indicate, the difference is perhaps due to the fact that Japanese firms' recruitment and selection had a higher degree of compatibility with Japanese cultural norms than German practice had with German cultural influences. Looking at the results this way it does seem advantageous for German firms to think well ahead about foreign assignment and recruitment as far as possible, in order to achieve cultural compatibility, rather than to follow the flexible and open approach suggested earlier (p.184). Moreover, if by this token the compatibility of recruitment and selection practice with a society's own cultural norms is a success factor, then we can conclude that the transfer of such practices is neither easy nor really necessary in terms of raising effectiveness through foreign management(30).

Notes

(1) M.H. Trevor, Japan's Reluctant Multinationals, Pinter, London, 1983.

(2) M. White, 'Japanese management and British workers', Public Policy, No.2. 1981, pp.49-58.

(3) J. Misumi and M. Peterson, 'The performance-maintenance (PM) theory of Leadership: Review of a Japanese Research Program', Administrative Science Quarterly, June 1985, pp. 198-223.

(4) A. Negandhi, 'Cross-cultural management research', Journal of International Business Studies, Fall 1983, pp.17-28.

(5) G. Hofstede, 'The cultural relativity of organisational practices and theories', Journal of International Business Studies, Fall 1985, pp.75-89.

(6) For the advantage of this concept in cross-cultural management theorising, see: U. Sekaran, 'Methodological and theoretical issues and advancements in cross-cultural research', Journal of International Business Studies, Fall 1983, pp.61-74. There are also, of course, problems connected with this concept. Unclear, for instance, is the relationship between the cultural dimensions. For a critique, see for instance: L. Goodstein, 'American business values and cultural imperialism' Organisational Dynamics, Summer 1981.

(7) Of course, management functions being complex, there may be some other underpinnings of recruitment besides the two mentioned as well. However, due to space considerations, an exemplary analysis should surfice here.

(8) H. Steinmann, B. Kumar and A. Wasner, 'Some aspects of managing US subsidiaries of German medium-sized enterprises', Management International Review, 3, 1979, pp.27-38.

(9) B. Baliga and A. Jaeger, 'Multinational corporations: Control systems and delegation issues', Journal of International Business Studies, Fall 1984, pp. 25-40.

(10) P. Kotler, L. Fahey and S. Jatusripitak, The New Competition, Prentice Hall, Englewood Cliffs NJ, 1985.

(11) S. Marsland and M. Beer, 'The evolution of Japanese management: Lessons for US managers, Organisational Dynamics, Winter 1980, pp. 49-67.

C. Yang, 'Demystifying Japanese management practices' Harvard Business Review, Nov-Dec. 1984, pp.172-182.

(12) K. Rüssmann, 'Konsens statt Konflikt', Manager Magazin, August 1981, pp.36-40.
Y. Zussmann, 'Learning from the Japanese: Management in a resource-scarce world', Organisational Dynamics, Winter 1983, pp.68-79.

(13) C. McMillan, The Japanese industrial system, De Gruyter, Berlin, 1984.

(14) Such loyalty does not of course exclude the possibility of interpersonal conflict and dissatisfaction. For this aspect of Japanese expatriates, see: B. Kumar and H. Steinmann, 'Führungskonflikte in deutsch-japanischen Management-Beziehungen', S.J. Park, U. Jürgens and P. Merz (eds.) Transfer des japanischen Managementsystems, Express Edition, Berlin, 1985, pp.133-154.

(15) H. Steinmann, B. Kumar and A. Wasner, op.cit.

(16) J. Hirscheimer, 'Management', H. Hammitzsch (ed.) Japan-Handbuch, Steiner, Wiesbaden, 2nd edn., 1984, cols.2239-2246.

(17) H. Steinmann and B.Kumar, 'Angst vor der Rückkehr' Manager Magazin, December 1976.

(18) This type of approach, where the ends-ways-means paradigm is turned on its head to a means-ways-end concept, is discussed in recent strategic management literature, for example: R. Hays, 'Expatriate selection. Insuring success and avoiding failure', Journal of International Business Studies' Spring 1974, pp. 25-38.

(19) H. Steinmann and B. Kumar, 'Personalpolitische Aspekte von im Ausland tätigen Unternehmen', E. Dichtl and D. Issing (eds.) Exporte als Herausforderung für die deutsche Wirtschaft, Deutscher Institutsverlag, Cologne, 1984.

(20) E. Dichtl, H. Kögelmayr and S. Müller, 'Die Unlust im Ausland zu arbeiten', Blick durch die Wirtschaft, 8 August 1983.

(21) H. Steinmann and B. Kumar, op.cit. 1984,

(22) P. Buckley and H. Mirza, 'The wit and wisdom of Japanese management: an iconoclastic analysis', Management International Review, Vol.25, 1985, pp.16-40.

(23) R. de Frank, M. Matterson, D. Schweiger and J. Ivancevich, 'The impact of culture on the management practices of American and Japanese CEOs', Organisational Dynamics, Spring 1985, pp.62-76.

(24) J. Stoner, J. Aram, and J. Rubin, 'Factors associated with

effective job performance in overseas work assignments', Personnel Psychology, 25, 1972, pp.303-318.

(25) For the detailed methodology and operationalisation of Maslow's need categories for expatriate assignments, see H. Steinmann and B. Kumar, 'Über die Arbeitszufriedenheit entstandter Führungskräfte deutscher Unternehmen im Ausland', H.-J. Engeleiter (ed.) Unternehman und Gesellschaft, Verlag Neue Wirtschaftsbriefe, Herne/Berlin, 1976, pp.121-141.

(26) In terms of the possibility of making friends, for example. Cf. L. Porter, 'A study of perceived need satisfaction in bottom and middle management jobs' Journal of Applied Psychology, 45, 1961.

(27) S. Marsland and M. Beer op.cit.

(28) This relationship has been investigated by Hays (op.cit., 1974).

(29) Such transfers of parent company personnel to subsidiaries have been noted lately, as in the course of increased international competition Japanese firms find it difficult to sustain lifelong employees. Cf. P. Sethi, N. Namiki and c. Swanson, 'The decline of the Japanese system of management', California Management Review, Summer 1984, pp.35-45.

(30) See also: R. Hays, 'Strategic planning - forward in reverse?' Harvard Business Review, November - December 1985, pp. 111-119. G. Hofstede, Culture's consequences: international differences in work-related values, Sage, Beverly Hill/London, 1980. J. Sheridan and J. Slocum, 'The direction of the causal relationship between job satisfaction and work performance', Organisational Behaviour and Human Performance, 14, 1975.

Table 1 Recruitment for overseas assignment

Method	Japanese in Germany N = 135	Germans in Japan N = 101*
Told by company to to take up job (ad hoc)	109 (80 %)	61 (60 %)
Own initiative	26 (20 %)	31 (31 %)
Mutually planned with company	-	12 (12 %)

*N = 101 due to multiple answers

Table 2 Motives for assigning parent company managers instead of local nationals in foreign subsidiaries

Why expatriates thought they were assigned (job requirements)	Germans in Japan* N = 101	Japanese in Germany* N = 135
- Transferring parent co's know-how, resources	1,70 (2)	1,91 (1)
- Integration of activity of subsid. into global strategy	1,56 (1)	2,02 (2)
- Establishing loyalty to parent co.	2,47 (3)	3,63 (6)
- Training local staff in parent co. practices	3,19 (4)	3,08 (3)
- Gaining foreign experience	3,33 (5)	3,51 (4)
Representing as foreign firm	3,42 (6)	3,64 (7)
- Easier communication with local customers	4,22 (7)	3,61 (5)

* Importance on a 5-point scale (1 = very important)

Table 3 Selection criteria and their perceived importance for overseas assignments

Selection criteria (in view of respondents)	Japanese in Germany* N = 135	Germans in Japan* N = 101*
Preparedness to take on (greater) responsibility	2,24 (3)	2,06 (1)
Knowledge of parent co. for know-how transfer and ability to coordinate activity	2,18 (1)	2,25 (2)
Ability to adapt knowledge to local conditions	2,22 (2)	2,61 (3)
Leadership ability	2,57 (5)	2,75 (4)
Foreign experience	3,14 (6)	2,88 (5)
Feeling of duty towards co.	2,48 (4)	-
Knowledge of local language	3,56 (7)	4,43 (7)
Willingness of wife/family to go	3,92 (8)	3,68 (6)

* Importance on a 5-point scale (1 = very important)

Table 4 Perceived job satisfaction of expatriates*

Need categories (Maslow)	Germans in Japan* N = 101	Japanese in Germany* N = 135
Self-actualisation (e.g. applying one's qualifications)	0,505	0,407
Social (e.g. making friends)	0,598	0,447
Status (e.g. respect inside/ outside co.)	0,306	0,556
Security (job security)**	0,52	-

* According to Porter's need deficiency questionnaire, the greater the score the greater the job dissatisfaction.

** Due to life-long employment in Japanese firms, the question proved irrelevant among Japanese expatriates.

Figure 1 The Position of the 50 Countries on the Power Distance and Uncertainty Avoidance Scales:

A POWER DISTANCE × UNCERTAINTY AVOIDANCE PLOT
for 50 countries & 3 regions

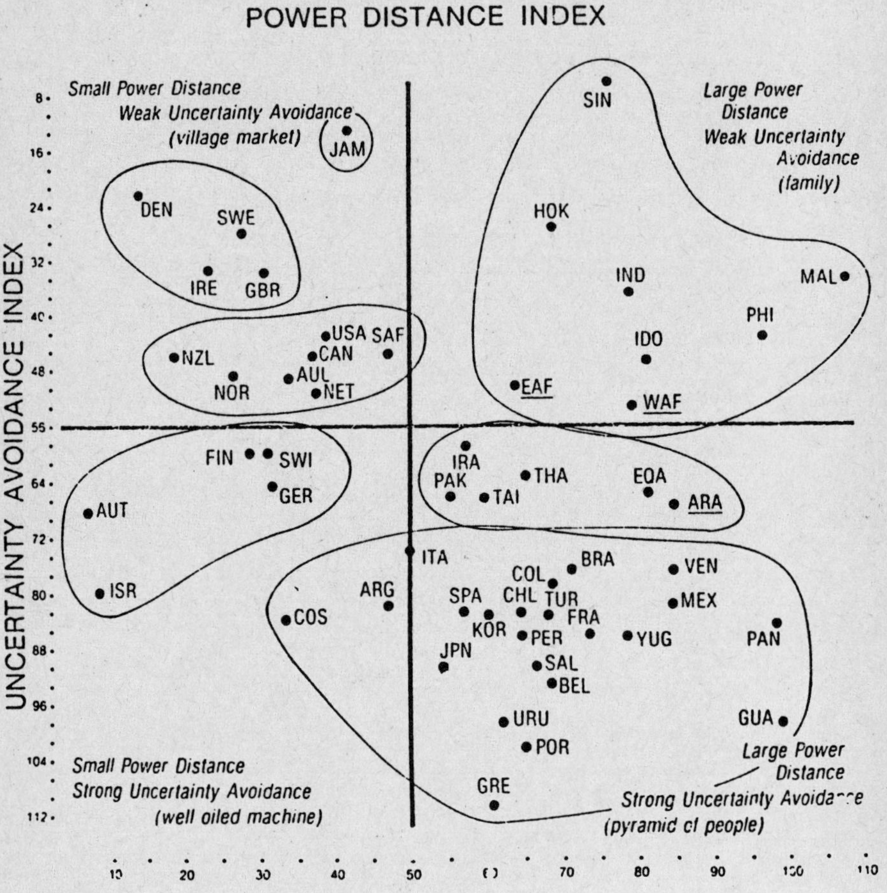

Source: Hofstede (1983)

Figure 2 A POWER DISTANCE × INDIVIDUALISM—COLLECTIVISM PLOT *for 50 countries & 3 regions*

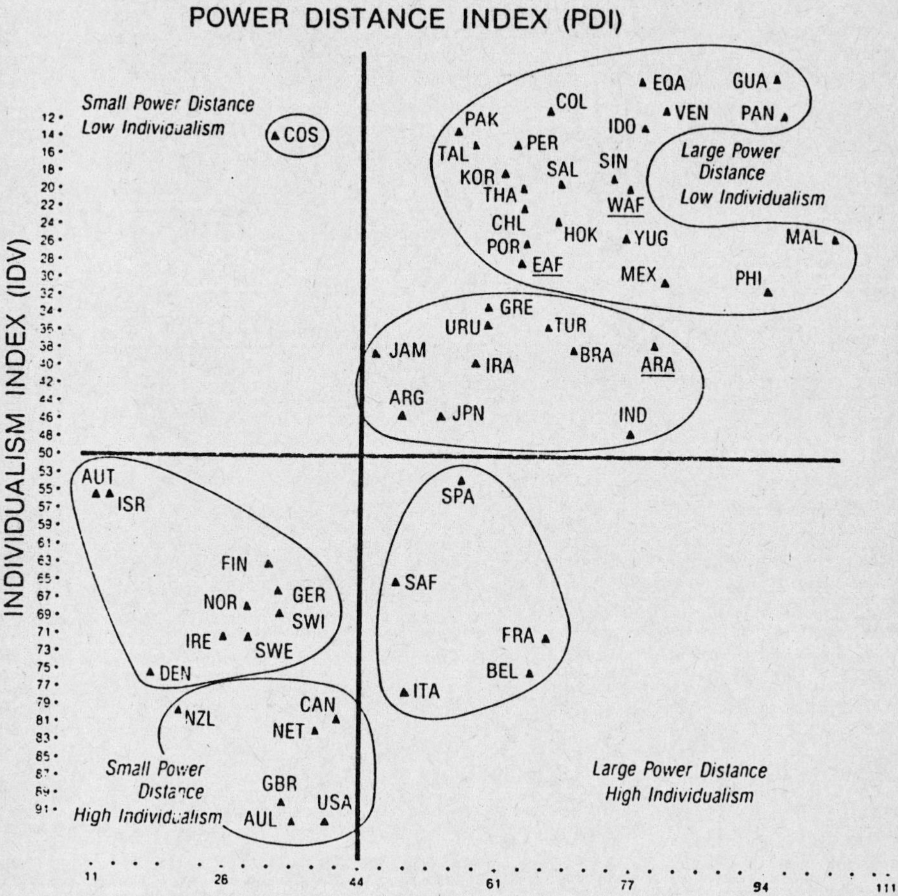

Source: Hofstede (1983)

JAPANESE DIRECT FOREIGN INVESTMENT IN THE NETHERLANDS: AN OVERVIEW

J. A. Stam
Erasmus University

The last decade and a half has shown an intensification of efforts to attract Japanese foreign investment. While in the early seventies Japanese corporations and financial institutions were seeking investment opportunities in the United States and Europe for their large surpluses incurred by a continuously profitable economic performance, since the early eighties the scope of direct foreign investment has broadened and governments are showing interest as well.

As has been argued by Kudo above(1), the Japanese government sees ample opportunities to internationalise the Japan economy and business by stimulating direct foreign investment, at home and abroad, and thus trying to diminish the pressure on Japan invoked by the long-lasting trade imbalances between Japan and the main advanced economic nations. Japanese companies on their side have their own arguments for direct investment in foreign countries. The pending threat of protectionism or market closure as a result of the distorted economic relations between Japan and the Western countries being one and overly discussed reason, long-term strategies for advanced products or the obvious need for joint efforts in technological development and industrial corporation being another. In addition, the investment opportunities offered by the respective governments seem to be most accommodating to the prospective investor.

European governments, and lately also American states' governments, have changed their policy of low profile acquisition of direct Japanese company investment into an active and sometimes even aggressive one. Embassies in Tokyo are bustling with activities and 'country marketing' has become the newest specialist tool. All these efforts are implicitly based upon the assumption that the presence of Japanese companies creates the jobs which are so desperately needed in Europe.

How successful have European countries been in attracting

Japanese business investments? Of the total Japanese foreign investment in the period 1951 to 1984, amounting to 71,431 billion US dollars, Europe has been able to attract 12.7 per cent, a fourth position behind North America (30.1 per cent), Asia (25.2 per cent) and even Latin America (18.2 per cent)(2). It should be noticed, however, that Europe's modest performance has improved and of the total Japanese foreign investment in 1984 (10,155 billion US dollars), 19.1 per cent was invested in European countries.

Within Europe the United Kingdom is with 31.2 per cent of the total 9,072 billion US dollars (1951-1984) the major host country for Japanese investors, followed by Germany (13.2 per cent) and in third place the Netherlands (12.1 per cent). In 1984 the Netherlands even appeared to have attracted the major share (23.3 per cent) of all Japanese investments in Europe. Taking the Dutch position into consideration, is there reason to be satisfied? Have all the efforts spent on promotion and acquisition been worthwhile? How many direct new jobs have been created?

As of December 1985 the Netherlands accounted for 156 Japanese establishments, ranging from simple agencies to full-fledged factories(3). These establishments employ 691 Japanese expatriates and 4,021 Dutch employees. Almost one third of all these Japanese establishments are small offices, occupied by a single Japanese expatriate, yielding no direct local employment but general income to the local economy. In terms of employment the category of 11-20 and 21-50 employees are most contributive. Large establishments are rare, although recent investments show a substantial growth potential both in terms of turnover and employment.

A breakdown in types of activities reveals the dominance of the service sector. Banks and finance houses, service centres for Japanese products, distribution centres for Japanese products for the European market, transportation and commerce score high, while there are only a few establishments in the industrial sector. Although the Japanese manufacturing companies employ advanced production technology, the many high-tech jobs which are needed are not yet being offered.

What could be the reason for the relatively low share of Japanese investment production facilities in the Netherlands? First of all, the competition for Japanese investment in Europe is intense. In spite of general regulations, national governments try to conclude deals and contracts on a bi-lateral basis, deploying economic, trade, political and strategic arguments to convice Japanese partners to invest in country A or region X instead of elsewhere. Secondly, the Netherlands as a home market for manufactured products has only a limited potential due to its size. Therefore, merchandise manufactured according to market specifications tends to be produced in countries with larger local markets as, for instance, West Germany, France the United Kingdom. A third reason why Japanese electronic industries in particular are reluctant to invest in the Netherlands is the presence of their main competitor, Philips. Although a multinational company with establishments throughout Europe, Japanese companies seem to hesitate to come close to the home turf of Philips. The often cited reason for their absence is the fact that Philips recruits the top of the educational market in electronics of the Netherlands on a massive scale which seriously interferes with the standing policy of top Japanese electronics makers to recruit the best engineers available. In addition, similar to the Japanese sub-contracting system with strong interdependencies between the parts manufacturer and the assembly company, Philips has improved its relationship with local parts makers. Under the label of co-makership Philips is providing technical assistance in design and production to sub-contractors and parts suppliers, thus trying to integrate and smooth out its own production system. Under these circumstances it could, indeed, be considered difficult for Japanese electronics makers to contract adequate local Dutch sub-contractors or parts suppliers for the production of Japanese goods in the Netherlands.

In spite of the structural or temporary impediments to large scale Japanese investment in production facilities in the Netherlands, overall performance in attracting Japanese investors can be considered satisfactory in view of the structure of the Dutch economy and the position of the Netherlands in Europe and in world markets. With an economy thriving on agricultural exports, trade, transportation, financial and commercial services it is only natural to attract similar types of foreign investment. So far the profitability of Japanese investments in the Netherlands has not been in question.

Notes

(1) See pp. 63 - 72 above.

(2) These data have been adopted from: H.P. Merz, S.J. Park, Japanisches Management in der Bundesrepublik Deutschland, Struktur und Strategien, Express Edition, Berlin 1986.

(3) Detailed information has been obtained from the respective governmental agencies pertaining to foreign direct investment in the Netherlands.

Table 1 Japanese direct investment in the Netherlands 1980-83
(In million guilders. As at 31 December of each year. Not cumulative)

Year	Agriculture & fishing	Industry	Service	Total
1980	1	31	562	594
1981	9	71	672	752
1982	2	57	1018	1077
1983	0	191	1100	1291

Source: M. van Nieuwkerk and R.P. Sparling, The international investment position of the Netherlands, (in Dutch). Deventer, 1985.

Figure 1 Employment contribution of 113 Japanese establishments in the Netherlands
(Area size indicates the number of companies providing employment to x-y number of employees.

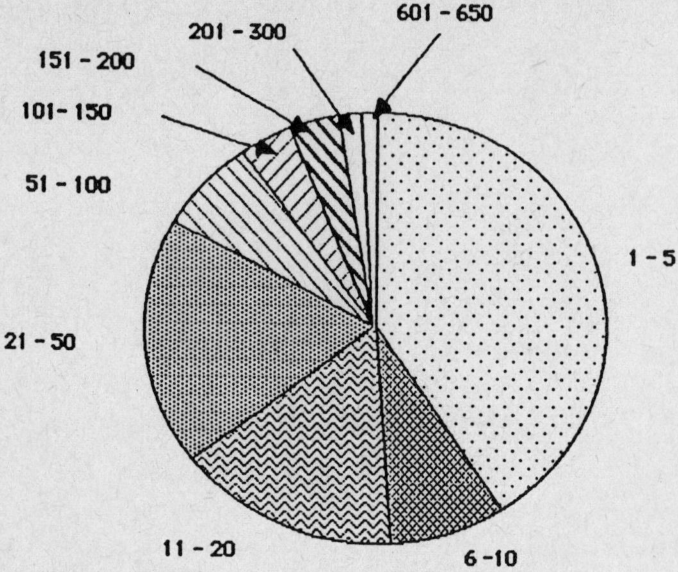

Employment by Japanese establishments

Order: 1

☒ Plot Series

Class size	Total number of companies
1 - 5	46
6 -10	9
11 - 20	18
21 - 50	21
51 - 100	8
101- 150	4
151 - 200	4
201 - 300	2
601 - 650	1

CONCLUSION

J.A. Stam
Erasmus University

During the two-day conference we listened to various contributions on the state of affairs concerning the internationalisation of Japanese business(1). The variety of participants from European and Japanese business, from academia, politics and governmental circles, both from Europe and Japan, guaranteed a wide spectrum of issues for discussion. The central problems related to the internationalisation of Japanese business, as they occurred during presentations and discussions, could be summarised as follows: problems related to the economic aspects of internationalisation, from commodity certification, capital transfer, enterprise management to trade friction and the like; problems related to cultural and psychological aspects of internationalisation, the phenomenon of 'the international manager' and the internationalisation of management styles; problems related to the internationalisation of society, the globalisation of economy and culture and the rising belief that internationalisation is equivalent to modernisation.

Based upon the papers and the ensuing discussions we can draw a map for research, partly filled in already, partly with open spaces. From a research point of view we can distinguish four areas of attention:

1. The nature of internationalisation

The term 'internationalisation' is commonly used in the context of 'interaction and exchange' between different nations. This phenomenon, ubiquitous in contemporary society, is, however, being emphasised in Japan to such an extent that the question becomes relevant: is this movement in Japan just the latest fashion, eventually withering away, or is it perhaps a real new stage in the development of relations between Japan and the outside world? If so, what is the meaning and content of internationalisation? In terms of semantics we could question the meaning of 'international'. The Japanese equivalent for the English word international is kokusai, the opposite to kokunai, meaning 'inside the country'. Does the Japanese work kokusai, literally meaning, 'outside the country/nation', indeed have the same connotation as 'international', denoting the relations **between** countries, or should we interpret kokusai as: all affairs not directly concerning Japan? If the latter would be the case we, consequently, could distinguish between, for example, two types of businessmen: the one dealing with internal, Japan-related affairs and possessing a powerful position, and the one conducting business with foreign countries, as an expatriate at a foreign establishment or in the international division at company headquarters. This semantic dichotomy between kokusai and kokunai, trivial as it may seem, could be of essential influence on the development of international relations between Japan and the outside world.

Apart from semantic connotations, internationalisation seems to have a distinct meaning in the eyes of the Japanese government. All efforts to internationalise the economy and society and improve relations implicitly intend to demonstrate to the outside world that Japan seriously wants to participate in the international community as a responsible nation. At industrial branch level, however, internationalisation could mean, for example, deciding on industrial standards for products, regulations on flows of commodities, exchange of technology and the like. For individual Japanese companies internationalisation could imply expansion of business activities, improvement of competitiveness of products and services. The basic question, however, related to the issue of internationalisation at company level is: which opportunities are envisioned by going international, or which threats are feared in case one decides not to do so? This leads us to a second area of attention.

2. The nature and content of Japanese business strategy

For a subject like business strategy we can draw upon rich sources in economic and management literature. American and European multinational companies have been analysed in great detail and recently Japanese companies have also been added to this score(2).

As a subject like strategy is very volatile and apt to change, continuous monitoring seems necessary. Questions likely to be raised, could be: are Japanese company strategies for internationalisation reactive or proactive? Are international activities triggered by a changing business environment, politically or economically, or are they part of a long-term, pre-designed plan? In other words, do Japanese companies follow deliberate strategies based upon a clear concept of expansion or can we notice only emerging strategies, piecemeal thinking incited by the actions of, for example, the main competitor in the market? Another question to be answered: does one consider the whole world as the market or is there any concentration in specific parts or areas, for example, the advanced industrial countries with their well-developed commercial infrastructure and high income consumer markets? As far as technology is concerned, there is of course the question: does one start in one's own market with advanced products and then move onwards to different, advanced markets, making use of the learning curve effect, or does one move from a simple technology market to a complex one by way of internationalisation, for instance, through mergers, joint ventures or participation in consortia(3)?

Of course, a fair amount of research has been conducted already on these matters and by now we have more than just a slight indication, but a continuous systematic study of the business strategies of Japanese companies investing in Europe remains necessary from the point of view of the trade, financing or manufacturing policies of the host countries.

3. The structure of Japanese business

Both in theory and practice strategy is paired off with structure. Given a certain strategy how do Japanese companies in Europe structure their operations? If we follow Mintzberg's line of thought that the structure of an organisation concerns the division of labour and the coordination of tasks, then we encounter a vast area for research with many 'empty' spots. Issues likely to be tackled here are formal and informal organisational structure, the decision-making authority of the foreign establishment (centralised/decentralised), the span of control of managers, the numbers of and relations between expatriate staff and local staff etc. Again, for this area of attention a fairly large amount of comparative material and adequate research methods are already available. The main problem in analysing the structural aspects of Japanese establishments in Europe is the 'fluidity' of the companies. This can be directly related to their relative youth and fast growth.

4. Actual operations of Japanese business establisments

A fourth area of attention for the analysis of the internationalisation of Japan business are the operations themselves. Since Japanese companies established themselves in Europe and started production plants or service organisations, they have aroused the interest of local competitors. As competitiveness, by all means, demonstrates itself mostly at the operational level, particularly when the conditions are comparable, detailed studies of day to day operations at shopfloor level, at supervisory level or managerial level on a comparative basis are extremely useful. In view of the different traditions in Japan and Western Europe, of course, industrial relations and personnel management practices are natural issues to be studied, but apart from these, analysis of other functional areas of the business organisation are welcome as well. To mention a few, the marketing and advertisement of local products, product design and market adjustment, relations with local part suppliers and sub-contractors, community-oriented activities and so on.

During the conference many of the issues mentioned above were dealt with by the respective speakers and discussants. As was proved during the meeting, research is making progress both in scope and in depth. However, two areas should be singled out for more detailed scrutiny. It seems to be justified to pay more attention to the analysis of the internationalisation strategy of the Japanese government and the ensuing strategies of Japanese corporations. If internationalisation implies lasting relations between countries and the integration of economic systems, then, in view of a joint design of the coming interdependency, a serious study of the path set out by Japan and Japanese companies is due. Particularly in the field of international economic relations, a 'wait and see' attitude could have highly disturbing effects on the development of new markets and new products. Secondly, at the micro level serious atttention should be paid to management-worker relations in Japanese companies in Europe. Since earlier research on this subject showed a great variety of approaches, a comparative study of different configurations of relations in respective companies could provide interesting clues to the problem of the 'best' fit to a monolithic bloc that encompasses many different traditions, styles and cultures in management. Comparisons should go beyond national borders and comprise configurations prevalent in different countries, differentiated according to type of activity, be it production, trade or finance, and also according to differences in the corporate cultures of the mother companies involved. Those to benefit from such a comparative study are not only the researchers or the local competitors but the Japanese companies as well. A systematic feedback on their operations and performance in comparison to local companies could yield the information for a proper assessment of their investment. Therefore, an appeal for cooperation and joint research seems to be in place. Since the interests of both Japan and Europe are at stake, the establishment of the

Euro-Japanese Management Studies Association combining the efforts of the business community, the respective governments and academia, has been a timely initiative with a promising future.

Notes

(1) These 'concluding observations' are an edited version of the author's 'summing up' at the end of the conference.

(2) See for instance publications like: Ozawa Terutomo, Multinationalism, Japanese Style, the Political Economy of Outward Dependency, Princeton, N.J., Princeton University Press, 1979; L.G., Franko, The Threat of Japanese Multinationals, London, Wiley & Sons, 1983;
M. White and M.H. Trevor, Under Japanese Management, The Experience of British Workers, London, Policy Studies Institute, 1983;
M. Takamiya and K.E. Thurley (eds.), Japan's Emerging Multinationals, An International Comparison of Policies and Practices, Tokyo, University of Tokeyo Press, 1985;
M.H. Trevor, Japanese Industrial Knowledge: Can It Help British Industry? London, Gower/PSI, 1985.

(3) In his recent book Triad Power, The Coming Shape of Global Competition, New York, Free Press, 1985, Ohmae Kenichi foresees the emergence of international consortia and syndicates to cope with financial and technological problems in advanced markets.

Notes on Contributors

Dr Malcolm Trevor is Director of the Japan Industrial Studies Programme at the Policy Studies Institute, the independent London-based research institute. A graduate of Oxford University, University College, London, and the London School of Economics, he lived and worked in Japan between 1962 and 1971. He has recently researched Japanese marketing. His current research concerns the making of the new company at Toshiba Consumer Products (UK) and the relations between Japanese manufacturers in the UK and the local British firms that supply them with components. He was elected Chairman of the Euro-Japanese Management Studies Association in 1985. He has published and spoken extensively on Japanese business at home and abroad.

Professor Sung-Jo Park is a graduate of Seoul National University, the Sorbonne and the Free University, Berlin, and is Professor in the East Asia Department of the Free University, Berlin. He has worked in Korea, Japan, the United States, Spain and Germany. Since 1983 he has been leading a team on research into Japanese investment in Western Europe, supported by the Volkswagen Foundation.

Dr Hans-Peter Merz completed his doctorate on Japanese companies in Germany at the Free University, Berlin, where he is engaged on the Japanese Management research project.

F.H. Saelens studied at the University of Manchester Institute of Science and Technology, where he completed a publication on Japanese investment in Europe. He is in the Corporate Planning Department of Philips at Eindhoven.

Professor Akira Kudo is Associate Professor of Economics at the University of Tokyo and has published on trade relations between Japan, Europe and USA.

Mr Mitsuya Goto is General Manager, Public Affairs, of Nissan's International Division, Tokyo. He is a graduate of the Woodrow Wilson School of International Relations, Princeton University, and has worked in Britain and Belgium.

Mrs Ritsuko Miyajima is a graduate of Keio University and the University of Manchester Institute of Science and Technology. Her research field is the interaction between British and Japanese managers and their mutual perceptions.

Dr Ulrich Jürgens is a Research Fellow at the Wissenschaftszentrum (Science Centre), Berlin, and a specialist on the motor industry. Hans-Peter Strömel is Personnel Director at Volkswagen.

Dr A.R. Prindl has degrees from Princeton, the University of Kentucky and the London School of Economics. After managing the Tokyo office of Morgan Guaranty, he became Managing Director of Nomura Securities in London and recently established Nomura International Finance Ltd.

Mr H.J. Heise works for Eurosurvey, the Wiesbaden personnel and recruitment consultants, and is writing a thesis on personnel management in Japanese companies in Germany.

Dr Knuth Dohse recently moved from the Wissenschaftszentrum, Berlin, where he specialised on research into the motor industry, to take up a post as personnel manager at Schering AG.

Mr Y. Abe completed his M.Sc. thesis on the internationalisation of Japanese pharmaceutical companies at the Manchester Business School. He has now returned to the headquarters of Yamanouchi Pharmaceutical Co. in Tokyo.

Professor Yoshiaki Takahashi is professor in the Faculty of Business Administration, Institute of Management Research, Chuo University, Tokyo.

Professor B. Kumar and Professor H. Steinmann teach International Business in the Department of Economics and Social Sciences at the University of Erlangen-Nuremberg. They have published on the relations between Japanese and German managers in Japanese companies in Germany.

Professor J.A. Stam heads the Department of Modern Japanese Studies at Erasmus University, Rotterdam. As well as at universities in the Netherlands, he has studied and researched at Keio University, Tokyo.